Playing Is Learning

A curriculum written for
Partners in Parenting Education

by

Perry M. Butterfield, M.A.
Senior Research Associate, Department of Psychiatry
Program for Early Developmental Studies
University of Colorado School of Medicine

Barbara Pagano, M.A.
Parent Educator, Overland High School

Sue F. Dolezal, M.A.
Teen Renaissance Program
Brighton District 27-J

Home Visitation Strategies adapted by
Pilar Baca, M.S.R.N. and JoAnn Robinson, Ph.D.
Prevention Research Center for Families and Children
Department of Pediatrics, University of Colorado School of Medicine

**This volume was made possible by a grant from
the Gary-Williams Energy Corporation.**

For training information, contact:
How to Read Your Baby/P.I.P.E.
303-864-5164

Published by
HOW TO READ YOUR BABY
1825 Marion Street
Denver, CO 80218
303-864-5247
© 1997

revised 1997
ISBN 1-889839-02-7

Acknowledgments

We wish to acknowledge Nancy Gary, whose professional insight, energy and wisdom continue to reach out with help to children and families. Nancy and the Gary-Williams Energy Corporation provided the support which has made this volume possible. It is with grateful thanks for their commitment that we are able to complete the trilogy of curricula for Partners in Parenting Education.

To Robert Emde, M.D., the ultimate mentor, and to the Program for Early Developmental Studies, we thank you for your patience and your support.

With special thanks to Mary Stansberry, the Child Care Director at the TLC Program, Overland High School, Aurora, Colorado, who shared her infinite wisdom about adolescent parents with us throughout the development of PIPE. Also, we wish to thank Melody Bohlender, Bright Horizons Program, Horizon High School, Brighton, Colorado, for sharing her creativity in developing and piloting the teaching strategies in the original Play Unit volume.

We gratefully acknowledge Nancy Ottem for her enduring effort in preparing this curriculum for publication and Gabriel and Jacinto Hernandez for the playful artwork which enlivens this volume.

We wish to acknowledge the valuable insights of theoreticians in Early Child Development such as Robert Emde, Nathan Fox, Robert Harmon, George Morgan, Joy Osofsky, Arnold Sameroff, Louis Sander, Liz Bates, Allan Sroufe, Daniel Stern, Edward Tronic, as well as the overriding perspectives of Bowlby, Chess, Piaget, Spitz, Waddington and Winnicott.

This work draws upon our combined experiences with our own children, the children we have taught, and families we have counseled throughout the years, all of whom have given us great wisdom and courage.

Playing Is Learning

PARTNERS IN PARENTING EDUCATION

The Partners in Parenting Education (PIPE) curriculum was written specifically for adolescent parents, or for parents who have had less than optimal parenting examples themselves. There are three Units covered within the PIPE curriculum:

1. *Listen, Listen, Listen*
   focuses on communication/regulation skills and the baby as an individual.

2. *Love Is Layers of Sharing*
   focuses on relationship building.

3. *Playing Is Learning*
   focuses on the importance of emotional stability for learning.

KEY CONCEPTS

Each Unit covers the conceptual perspectives which we deem most valuable to parenting and which we feel are in need of a more complete representation in parenting curricula. These ideas are embedded in the framework of all of the Units and help educators to present - in differing contexts - a core of ideas that build good family relationships and confident, effective children.

These core concepts are

- **Emotional Development: the power of shared positive emotions**
- **Regulation: behavior management through mutual regulations and calm, quiet discipline**
- **Temperament: individual differences and individualized parenting**
- **Autonomy: respecting the child's view, developing mastery skills and scaffolding techniques**
- **Communication Skills: listening, language and problem solving, relationship building**
- **Personal Space: how parents can refresh and renew**

The Topics in the three Units are intended to cover the developmental period from birth to three years. All concepts are presented in a topical format and will apply to babies across this age span. This will allow you to select topics that are appropriate for your parents and to mix lessons across Units if you feel this is appropriate.

KEY TECHNIQUES

A few key techniques will help to ensure greater success for the parents involved. By structuring your teaching to include these steps, you and your parents will be rewarded.

1. Introduce material in small steps. Develop and practice one idea at a time.

2. Use Baby as teacher. Focus parent on the baby, speak through the child, encourage empathy for the child's position with each lesson.

3. Include an experiential learning experience, a supervised interaction, with each lesson.

Playing Is Learning

This Unit is about learning. It is about how babies learn and how parents can help or hinder this process. For many reasons, we have focused the Unit on the power of play to promote learning.

We believe that play is a natural corridor for learning in the first three years.

> Throughout nature the young are playful. For most mammals, playful activities involve practice in social and survival skills. Human babies also are learning through play to survive within their group. They are driven to master developmental milestones, and to copy and please the adults in their world. When learning is shared through play experiences, learning becomes paired with pleasure. Rules are accepted; there is pride in mastery and joy in sharing.

We know that shared positive emotions provide emotional stability and resilience.

> Parents who use positive emotion to regulate and educate their babies have babies that show love and respect and are able to use adults as resources. These babies demonstrate a positive identity and usually expect to participate in social interactions. They are less fussy and oppositional. They focus well and usually have good sleeping habits. We also know that children do better in school if their parents have used "interest" words and "teaching" statements to shape their first few years.

> Positive and negative emotions are processed by different neurological pathways. As in all early development, these pathways are strengthened with practice. As they are strengthened, they become firmly established as patterns of relationship which can last for a lifetime. By learning to interact with more positive emotions than negative, parents will set patterns that will shape the identity and self esteem of their baby.

Relationship patterns set in the first three years are predictive of a child's future success.

> Relationships in the first year are usually about safety, trust and love. In the second year relationships include rules, limitations, and confrontation. There is a marked spurt in babies' initiative toward the end of the first year. Babies are exploring more spaces and things but they are also exploring relationships: "What happens when I fuss, break a rule, or run away?" At this time, babies' emotions are uncontrolled; they cannot seem to regain balance. They are learning and changing in almost every mode of development at the same time. No day is the same.

How parents manage this spurt in initiative and the emotional extremes which occur throughout the second year will influence the pattern of their relationship with their baby for the rest of their time together. Also, this relationship pattern will set the guidelines for how babies will "fit in" with other family and childcare providers. This period is when babies learn tactics for surviving and sharing while still satisfying their own needs and wants. This is when babies learn to negotiate their drive for mastery with their drive to belong: "How do I gain independence and still stay close to my safe base?" It is parents who define this balance.

Play is a way to move smoothly and lovingly into the rules of pro-social behavior. Play teaches cooperation, collaboration, turn-taking, and rules. Play involves helping and sharing. Specific patterns or routines are set to achieve goals. Learning and mastery are inherent in play. Initiative can be expressed, yet channeled. And best of all, intimacy—or a feeling of acceptance—is fulfilled.

Toddlers need special understanding and special parenting tactics. They are demanding independence, testing their power, experiencing extremes of excitement, anger, and fear. At the same time, they are needing protection, seeking comfort, or collapsing with exhaustion. They are searching for models to help them understand how to behave and how to gain control of themselves. Toddlers need the closeness of a safe emotional base for balance.

The period from one to three years is notably difficult for all parents. Toddlers need some kind of co-regulation and guidance every five to ten minutes during their waking day. For high risk parents, this demanding period often turns into an angry battleground. Abuse or rejection during this period is not uncommon. Play and shared positive emotions are excellent tactics to teach parents.

Adolescent and high risk parents play less with their babies.
Some are embarrassed; others feel that playing is indulgent or wasteful effort. Some have been teased or assaulted during experiences which were initiated as play. Many have had little experience with play; they do not know how to play with an infant. They do not know what skills the baby is capable of learning. They do not know how to judge a baby's abilities or offer age-appropriate interactions. Expectations are set too high. There is little patience with the repetition and experimentation a baby uses to master skills.

Teaching parents how to play and how to teach through play will give them a skillful and enjoyable approach to managing the infant/toddler years. By increasing parents' understanding of ... how babies learn ... how they develop ... what their emotional, physical, and social needs are ... and how their behavior can be regulated without anger, they will be helped to establish positive relationship patterns with their babies. This leads to stable and resilient children.

Building Blocks for Play

Play Unit Topics

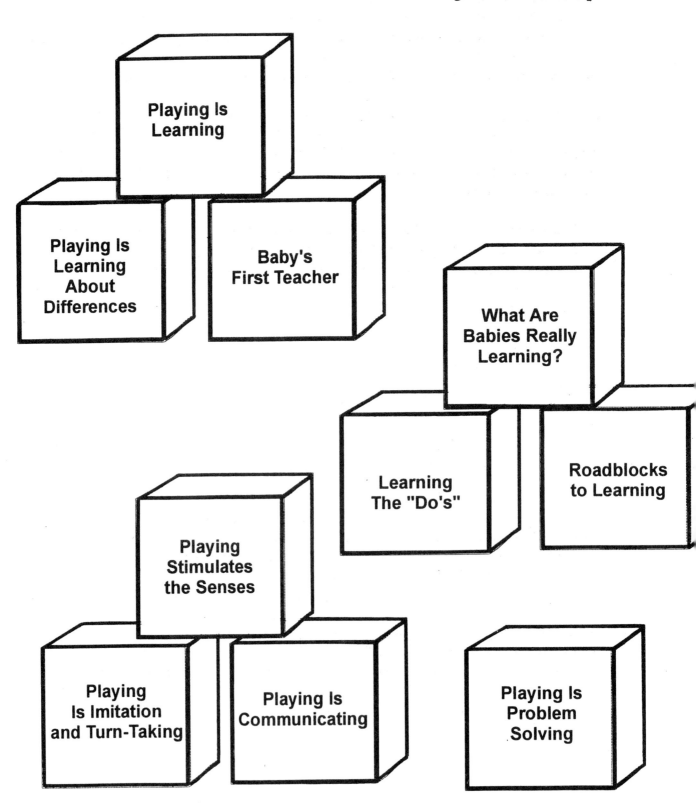

Introduction to *Playing Is Learning* Topics

Building Blocks and Building Strengths are themes for this Unit.

1. Use "Building Blocks for Play" to make a large poster and handouts.

2. Present <u>OVERVIEW</u>: This unit is designed to help parents understand how play is related to learning so that they will become more creative in the types of play activities they engage in with their babies. Topics will focus on why to encourage and scaffold developmentally appropriate play, why parents should join with their babies in play and how play activities can be used to regulate babies. Parents will learn how to become partners and guides for their babies' learning. (Illustrate this overview by using a set of children's blocks decorated to represent each topic. Explain how each block represents the facets of playing and learning. Stack the blocks to illustrate how each parent will use the information in this Unit to build a structure for learning which is unique to their relationship with their babies. Parents could color each block on their handout as it is explained.

Topic 1 Playing Is Learning Play is an important way babies learn. It combines fun and socialization while improving a skill or experiencing something new. Babies have an internal motivation to learn. Babies show this through their constant practice of a new skill. Exploration leads babies to discovery and mastery. Once they have it mastered, they move quickly to the next new learning task.

Topic 2 Playing Is Learning About Differences Play is a good way to see the individual in each baby. Each baby learns in different ways and at different rates. It is through observing and participating in play that parents can stay "in tune" with baby's development and readiness to learn.

Topic 3 Baby's First Teacher Parents are baby's first teacher. It is important for parents to seize the teachable moment. Learning and fun can take place in almost any situation. The daily "grind" can become more fun for both parent and baby when a routine turns into something interesting to learn. Parents will gain skills to become a good teacher.

Topic 4 What Are Babies Really Learning? Stabilization and socialization are the most important lessons of the first three years. Parents provide a stable base and an emotional connection for babies to gain equilibrium and begin learning. During the second year, parents become the model for toddlers to learn how to live with and enjoy other people. Play activities can help toddlers learn how to manage emotions and deal with frustrations.

Topic 5 Learning the Do's Play is one way babies learn how to "fit in" and behave. When play includes sharing positive emotions, babies are more willing to collaborate, cooperate and to follow the rules. Toddlers enjoy showing off their knowledge of the rules.

Topic 6 Roadblocks to Learning Sharing positive emotions and experiences encourages and sustains learning. Negative emotions, such as anger, can interfere with babies' learning. Parents will learn to use clear, calm, controlled negative messages to set limits.

Topic 7 Playing Stimulates the Senses All learning is through the senses. Touching, tasting, smelling, seeing, hearing and moving are sensory experiences. Playing enhances sensory experiences and balances learning. As babies touch a block, kick it, taste it, look at it, smell it or try to roll it, they understand more about it. Parents give these experiences meaning by modeling and guiding.

Topic 8 Playing Is Imitation and Turn-Taking Babies learn from watching and copying their parents. Imitation games are their first form of play. They will copy parents when they mouth, lip smack or stick out their tongue. When baby drops a toy on the floor, parent picks it up, gives it back to baby and baby drops it again, he is learning to take turns. Turn-taking is a form of imitation that teaches language, cooperation, and the basics of sharing.

Topic 9 Playing Is Communicating Play is a way babies learn to share feelings, ideas and knowledge. Playing together can help parent and baby establish a positive communication pattern. Communicating during activities, such as finger plays or reading books, also helps babies learn language.

Topic 10 Playing Is Problem Solving Babies develop problem solving skills when they master a task and feel competent and proud. When babies are struggling to solve a problem, it is sometimes hard for parents to let them do it themselves, but a parent's role is to set the stage and provide the support for the baby to have success. Then a parent can share in the baby's pride.

Directions/Procedures for the P.I.P.E. Interactive Session

Supervised Interaction in Home Visits or Parent Groups:

1. Parent prepares a private, quiet area, selects materials or toys appropriate to baby for this activity.

2. Parent interacts with baby, practicing the activity. The home visitor or experiential lab supervisor scaffolds a successful interactive session for parent and baby.

3. After session, parent puts materials away, letting baby help if possible.

4. Parent returns baby to nursery or other safe place, transitioning baby to another activity.

5. Parent completes ✦ "Topic Activity Sheet" (see Appendix).

FOR HOME VISITORS

The purpose of this activity is for parent and baby to have a positive interaction and to practice the topic skill.

Hopefully, interactive sessions can be scheduled when the household is quiet and the parent can give full attention to the baby. If there are other family members who want to watch and the parent agrees, this can be beneficial, but the parent should not be distracted from giving full attention to the baby.

Set a routine which parent and extended family will expect to follow, i.e. turn off TV, plan baby's schedule, etc.

A TIME SCHEDULE FOR PARENT GROUPS

10 Min. - Parents report to instructional area for clarification and review of the goals of the activities. Prepares area for baby.

5 Min. - Parent gets baby from child care room and brings to instructional area.

10+ Min.- Parent and baby participate in the activities. Continue until baby closes the activity.

5 Min. - Parent returns baby to child care area.

10+ Min.- Parent returns to instructional area evaluates the outcome of the activity and its application to the topical concepts. Puts equipment and toys away.

A Word To Our Parent Educators ...

PIPE is about emotional development, emotional connectedness, and emotion regulation. We believe that this is the basis of all successful parent child relationships and for the continued resiliency and competence of the child.

This Unit is focused more toward the Toddler. The interactive sessions and the play activities are often suggested for the 15- to 36-month-old. The information sheets for parents are also primarily about understanding the motivations of a toddler and skills for teaching and managing the socialization process.

We are delighted to have in this volume the Teaching Strategies for Home Visitors as well as for Parent Education Groups. These strategies have been adapted and piloted for two years by the Home Visitors and Supervisors from Home Visitation 2000, a research project directed by David Olds at the Prevention Research Center for Family and Child Health, University of Colorado School of Medicine, Department of Pediatrics.

Home Visitation 2000 integrates the three PIPE Curriculum Texts when teaching the PIPE techniques. This allows them to use the Topics in a more developmental format. For example, one could start with the Listen Text using topics about States of Awareness, State Regulation and Baby Cues, then move to the Love Text for Topics about Trust, Temperament, and Touch. By now the baby may be about 6 months old, and the Play Text (this volume) would be helpful to teach about Mastery, Development and the Senses. This would lead back to the Listen Text and "Music and Rhythm."

As you can see from this example, the PIPE Topics are interchangeable. Each Topic can be taught when your class or client is ready for this information. Each Topic can also be taught " in part," returning to teach more Key Concepts from a Topic at a later date. The PIPE curriculum is meant to be adaptable to your specific needs. We urge you to use this information to enhance your program and to integrate your other favorite teaching strategies or videos into the format.

The intent of the PIPE method is to strengthen and expand positive parent-child interactions. During the PIPE lessons, we urge you to focus your class or client on the interactive process, not on parent problems or family life issues. These issues can be addressed in other groups or counseling sessions designed for this.

We hope that the PIPE program will represent a tool for you to connect with your students and see change in their attitude, their skills, and their behavior.

CONCEPTUAL PLAN : Playing Is Learning

Session/Topic	Key Concepts	Demonstration	Interactive Session
1. Playing Is Learning	Play is a natural pathway for learning; play makes learning fun. Learning starts at birth. It is triggered by an internal motivation to explore and to master the new and different. Mastery leads to feelings of competence and pride. This is what drives us toward learning. Parents learn why babies need exploration and play to learn. Parents provide safe and interesting places to explore and to play.	The Blocks of Pride technique, structuring for autonomy and mastery during play.	Parents learn the PIPE interactive routine and the Blocks of Pride technique.
2. Playing Is Learning About Differences	Play defines differences. Through play, parents see change in their babies' development, temperament, and emotional needs. Learning about developmental milestones helps parental expectations. "Readiness to Learn," the "Personal Developmental Profile," and the "Emotional Seesaw" are concepts parents will use to enhance baby's learning and modify extremes of behavior.	Show babies' reactions to developmentally appropriate and inappropriate play.	Parents select toys using their babies' developmental profile to play with their baby.
3. Baby's First Teacher	Parents are the baby's first teacher. They are the most consistent and the most powerful teachers. They set and reinforce life patterns. Parents will learn how to create "teachable moments" and use the Teaching Loop. They will recognize their role as a model.	Demonstrate "Teachable Moments" using the Teaching Loop during a caregiving routine.	Prarents practice using the Teaching Loop during a caregiving routine.
4. What Are Babies Really Learning?	What are babies really learning? Babies learn most through their relationships with parents. They learn to stabilize and balance nerves and emotions through the protection, consistency and patterns of parents. They learn social skills and cultural norms using parents as a model and guide. Teaching styles are important. Parents learn how to mentor, coach, support and scaffold learning.	Demonstrate the Scaffolding Technique for supporting and expanding baby's interest and learning.	Parents practice using Scaffolding Technique in an activity with baby.
5. Learning the "Do's"	Learning the Do's helps baby be accepted in the family group. Babies must learn the do's and don'ts of behavior. They learn the rules and goals of their parents. Parents will learn the power of Shared Positive Emotions (SPE) in managing behavior. They will learn to change "don'ts" into "do's" and to use the "We" word in teaching and managing toddlers.	Demonstrate the use of SPE to change behavior, to extend play or to focus baby.	Parents practice using SPE to teach the rules (do's) of an activity.
6. Roadblocks to Learning	Negative emotions are roadblocks to learning. Shared emotions influence learning. Sharing positive emotions motivates learning; sharing negative emotions inhibits learning. Anger and teasing are hazards. Parents will learn skills for controlling anger and how to teach the "don'ts" without anger. Parents learn techniques for "quiet discipline" and enforcing limits with love.	Using SPE and clear, calm limits, show how to focus and regulate baby while reading a book.	Parents practice reading to baby using SPE and clear, calm limits to focus baby.
7. Playing Stimulates the Senses	All learning happens through sensory experience. Babies are learning about themselves and others through their senses. Parents will learn how play stimulates babies' senses, and how different sensory experience balances development and learning. They learn about sensory overload and how shared sensory experiences (rhythm, touching, voice tones) can regulate sensory overload.	Demonstrate sensory responses in baby using cotton massage or varieties of music.	Parents practice using a sensory game with their babies. They observe babies' reactions.

Session/Topic	Key Concepts	Demonstration	Interactive Session
8. **Playing Is** **Imitation &** **Turn-Taking**	The first form of play is imitation. As early as three months, babies copy parents' mouthing and sound games. Imitation leads to learning. Babies imitate parents' emotions also. Turn-taking teaches rules; rules help socialize babies. There is good and bad imitation. Parents will understand the dangers of bad imitation and discuss TV and other models in Baby's life. Imitation and turn-taking help babies learn language. Pretend is a form of imitation. Parents will learn how pretend helps babies with emotional development.	Demonstrate a turn-taking activity with a baby.	Parents practice an imitation or turn-taking activity with their babies.
9. **Playing Is** **Communicating**	Play encourages communication. Parents will learn skills and barriers for good communication. They learn the value of play to teach language and negotiation. Parents will learn how finger plays and rhythm get baby's attention. They learn how to read to a baby, and how books teach language and convey ideas and emotions. Parents use finger plays and books to redirect behavior.	Demonstrate finger plays to show how turn-taking games encourage communication with babies.	Parents practice communication skills using finger plays or books.
10. **Playing Is** **Problem Solving**	Play is a way to learn to problem solve. Parents will learn to make problems fun, divide them into small steps, when to let baby work on the problem and when to become a resource person for baby. Parents will learn that pretend is a way to try different solutions to a problem. They learn how to teach baby solutions by joining into pretend games.	Use the scaffolding technique to show developmental differences in teaching problem solving to a baby.	Using problem solving activities, parents practice scaffolding babies' success.
Conclusion:	Parents are the first and most important teachers for babies. They set the pattern, the focus, and the interest for babies' learning. They can maintain and enhance babies' natural motivation to explore and master, or they can inhibit and stifle it. By understanding how babies learn, what motivates them, and the power of emotional connectedness, parents will understand how play leads to learning and can make learning life-long fun.		

Following are symbols used in this Volume to guide the educator in using the materials. These symbols appear throughout the Concepts, Instructional Strategies, Demonstrations, Interactive Sessions and Topic Enhancers to inform the educator of worksheets and information pages which follow.

❖ Denotes the Key Concept you will be teaching.

◆ Denotes that suggested material appears on the following pages of the Topic.

☆ Denotes the activity to be completed during the Interactive Session.

Sometimes it is possible to teach two Key Concepts in one lesson. Most Topics will take several sessions to complete. Topics from other PIPE volumes can be interspersed with these Topics in order to adapt the material to a developmental format or to individualize it for Home Visitation or a specific clientele.

> For Home Visitors: The subject of discipline is a major concern to many home visitors. As home visitors, you have the opportunity to work individually with parents and to address the authoritarian styles which are detrimental to the equilibrium and socialization of the infant and toddler. Every Topic in this volume defines skills for regulating behavior and for avoiding behavioral difficulties. For those who want to invest your parent/client(s) in a more direct discussion of discipline, each Topic also includes a worksheet to open the discussion. These pages are called "DOOZYS: What *do* babies *do* to un-*do* Parents?" They are found in the appendix and are suggested for use as "Topic Enhancers."

MATERIALS AND SUPPLIES
for

Teaching Concepts

- Video recorder, VCR, & television

- Medium-sized empty box and several small boxes

- Assortment of art & craft supplies (construction paper, markers, glue, scissors, etc.)

- Parent & baby magazines

- Musical instruments (kazoos, xylophones, spoons, whistles, drums, bells, etc.)

- Tape of nursery songs and of different kinds of music and a tape player

- Simple pegboard or cardboard box & 6 dowels

- Pictures of facial expressions (parents & baby)

- Puppets or supplies to make puppets

- Materials & supplies to create the "Road to Learning" simulation, pg. 126, *Play* volume

- Age-appropriate books for babies

- Assorted candies (M & Ms, Life Savers, etc.)

- Blindfolds, small paper cups

- Cotton or feather for massage

- Strands of yarn, twine or pipe cleaners

- Small sticky note pads, baby puzzle

ACTIVITY CARDS

- Rattle, nesting cups

- Large, unbreakable mirror

- Assorted baby toys, soft doll, big blocks, toy cars & trucks, squeaky toy, small bell, pop-up box

- Baby blanket, patchwork quilt

- Two toy telephones

- Play dough, oatmeal

- Sheets of paper, sandpaper, crayons

- Long board, 3-4" wide

- Dish pan for water, soft sponges, towel, cookie cutters, foil pie tins, muffin tin, 6 tennis balls

- Pen light, 2 flashlights, feather duster

- Color strip paint samples

- 6 small plastic bottles

- Pans; wooden, metal & plastic spoons

- Texture ball or roller

- Elastic wrist bands with bells

- Texture glove, music box, spicy sox, Poke Box, color paddles, texture sticks (see instructions in *Play* volume appendix)

- Stuffed animal tied to elastic 1" beads, boot laces

- Soft, dry paint brush

- Wad of masking tape, sticky side out

RESOURCES: Playing Is Learning

Books and Pamphlets

Bailey, R. and E. Burton. <u>The Dynamic Infant</u>. St Paul, MN: Toys 'n Things Press, 1989.

Brisbane, H.E. <u>The Developing Child</u>. Peoria, IL: Glencoe, 1988.

Sendak, M. <u>Where the Wild Things Are</u>. USA: Harper & Row, 1963.

Sparling, G. and I. Lewis. <u>Learning Games for the First Three Years</u>. New York: Berkeley Books, 1979.

Developmental Tests — Choose 1 or 2

Bricker, D., Squires, J. and L. Mounts. <u>Ages and Stages: A Parent-completed Child-monitoring System</u>. Baltimore, MD: Paul Brooks Publishing, 1995. [Also available in Spanish.]

Frankenburg, W. and J. Dodds. <u>The Denver II</u>. Denver, CO: Denver Developmental Materials, 1990.

Furuno, S., O'Reilly, K., Hosaka, C., Zeisloft, B., and T. Allman. <u>Hawaii Early Learning Profile</u> (HELP). Palo Alto, CA: Vort Corporation, 1984.

Ireton, H. <u>Child Development Inventory</u> (CDI). Minneapolis, MN: Behavior Science Systems, Inc.

Reuter, J. and L. Bickent. <u>The Kent Infant Development Scale</u> (KID). Kent, OH: Kent Developmental Metrics, 1985.

Videos

Ambrose Video Production. <u>Childhood: Love's Labor</u>. A WNET co-production: 1290 Avenue of the Americas, Suite 2245; New York, NY 10104, 1987.

*Butterfield, P.M. & K.C. Connell. <u>Listen, Listen, Listen</u>, PIPE Video and Discussion Guide, Read Your Baby Videotape Series (1992).

*Butterfield, P.M. & K.C. Connell. <u>Love Is In the Palm of Your Hand</u>, PIPE Video and Discussion Guide, Read Your Baby Videotape Series (1992).

*Butterfield, P.M. & K.C. Connell. <u>Playing Is Learning</u>, PIPE Video and Discussion Guide, How to Read Your Baby Videotape Series (1992).

California Department of Education, Child Development Division and the Far West Laboratory for Educational Research and Development, Center for Child and Family Studies Discoveries of Infancy: Cognitive Development and Learning Video. Module III: Learning and Development. <u>Discoveries of Infancy: Cognitive Development and Learning</u>. 560 J. Street, Suite 220, Sacramento, CA, 96814. (800-445-7216 or 916-322-6233), 1995.

Videos, continued

Fewell, R. My Turn, Your Turn. CDMRC, University of Washington, Seattle, WA.
    (206-543-4011 x150), 1986.

Fowler, Wm., Ph.D. Talking from Infancy - How to Nurture & Cultivate Early Language.
    Produced by Wm. Fowler, Ph.D., Director of Center for Early Learning and Child Care
    in Cambridge, MA. [Available through Child Development Media Inc.]

Karl Lorimor Home Video. Parents Video Magazine: Baby Comes Home, Vol. 1.
    USA Publishing, 1986.

Milan Herzog Associates. Play. Developing Child Video Series, Magna Systems, Barrington, IL.
    (701-382-6477), 1994.

Milan Herzog Associates. Toddlerhood, Emotional Development. Developing Child Video Series,
    Magna Systems, Barrington, IL. (701-382-6477), 1994.

Activity Cards

*How to Read Your Baby/PIPE Activity Cards - Playing Is Learning, How Babies Learn Love,
    and Listen, Listen, Listen. A How to Read Your Baby Publication, Denver, CO, 1994.

    *Available only through Read Your Baby/PIPE, at 1825 Marion Street, Denver, CO 80218

Bibliography
Additional Resources for Educators and Parents

Bates, E., M. Beeghley-Smith, I. Bretherton, & S. McNew (1982). Social basis of language development: In H. Reese & L. Lipseet (eds.), *Advances in child development and behavior* (Vol. 16, pp. 8-75). New York: Academic Press.

Bates, E., B. Oconnell, & C. Shore (1987). Language and communication in infancy. In Osofsky, J. (ed.) *Handbook of infant development* (second edition). John Wiley, New York, pp. 149-203.

Beck, Ian and Sarah Williams. *Ride-A-Cock Horse.*

Bowlby, J. (1988). *A secure base—Parent-child attachment and healthy human development.* New York: Basic Books.

Castle, Katherine, Ed.D. *The Infant Toddler Handbook.* Atlanta, GA: Humanics Limited, 1983.

Cicchetti, D., J. Ganiban, & D. Barnett (1991). Contributions from the study of high-risk populations to understanding the development of emotion regulation. In J. Garber & K.A.Dodge (eds.), *The development of emotion regulation and dysregulation.* Cambridge: Cambridge University Press.

Cryer, Debby, T. Harms and B. Bourland. *Active Learning for Infants* and *Active Learning for Ones.* Redding, MA: Addison-Wesley, 1987.

Cole, C. and S. Calmenson (1991). *Eentsy, Weensy Spider.* New York: Mulberry Books.

Emde, R.N. (1980). Emotional availability: A reciprocal reward system for infants and parents with implications for prevention of psychosocial disorders. In P.M. Taylor (ed.), *Parent-infant relationships* (pp. 87-115). Orlando, FL: Grune & Stratton.

Emde, R.N., Z. Biringen, R.B. Clyman, and D. Oppenheim (1991). The moral self of infancy: Affective core and procedural knowledge. *Developmental Review,* 11, 251-270.

Emde, R.N. (1991). Positive emotions for psychoanalytical theory: surprises from infancy research and new directions. *Journal of the American Psychoanalytic Association.* International Universities Press, Inc. Madison, CT.

Emde, R.N. editor (1996). Zero to Three: National Center for Infants, Toddler, and Families. Special issue on intervention, prevention, and social emotional development using Partners in Parenting Education as a focus. *Bulletin* 17(1).

Fox, N.A. (1994). The development of emotion regulation: biological and behavioral considerations. *Monographs of the Society for Research in Child Development*, 59 (2-3, Serial No. 240).

Goldberg, S., R. Muir, & J. Kerr (1995). *Attachment theory: Social, developmental and clinical perspectives.* Hillsdale, NJ & London: The Analytic Press.

Greenborough, Wm. T., J.E. Black, & C.S. Wallace (1987). Experience and brain development. *Child Development* 58, 539-559. Society for Research in Child Development, Inc.

Klass, Carol Speekman (1996). *Home Visiting: promoting healthy parent and child development*. Paul Brookes. Baltimore.

Klaus, M. and P. Klaus (1985). *The Amazing Newborn*. Redding, MA: Addison-Wesley Publishing Company.

Lansky, V. *Games Babies Play* (1993). Deephaven, MN: The Book Peddlers.

Linder, T. *Transdisciplinary Play-Based Assessment* (1990). Baltimore, MD: Paul H Brookes Publishing Company.

MacTurk, R.H., and George Morgan (eds.) (1995). Mastery Motivation, Origins, Conceptualizations and applications. *Advances in applied developmental Psychology*, Vol. 12. Ablex Publishing, Norwood, NJ.

McClure, V.S. (1989). *Infant Massage*, New York: Bantam Books.

Olds, David, and Jon Korfmacher, Guest Editors (Jan. 1997). Special Issue on Home Visitation. Journal of individual differences in children's cognitive competence. *Developmental Psychology*, 20, 166-179.

Piaget, J. (1952). *The origins of intelligence in children* (M. Cook, Trans.). New York: International Universities Press. (Original work published 1936).

Pipp, S., M.A. Easterbrooks, and R.J. Harmon (1992). The relation between attachment and knowledge of self and mother in one- to three-year-old infants. *Child Development*, 63, 738-750.

Sander, L.W. (1962). Issues in early mother-infant interaction. *Journal of the American Academy of Child Psychiatry*, 1, 141-166.

Silberg, J. (1993). *Games to Play with Babies*. Mt. Ranier, MD: Gryphon House.

Sroufe, L. Alan (1996). *Emotional development: the organization of emotional life in the early years*. Cambridge University Press.

Tronick, E. (1989) Emotions and emotional communication in infants. *American Psychologist*, 44, 112-119.

Werner, E.E. and R.S. Smith (1982). *Vulnerable but invincible: A study of resilient children*. New York: McGraw-Hill.

For Parents:

Ames, Louise B. & Francis L. Ilg (1980). *Your Two-Year-Old: Tender or Terrible*. Delacorte Press, New York.

Lieberman, Alicia F. 91993). *The Emotional Life of the Toddler.* New York, Free Press.

Shatz, Marilyn (1994). *A Toddler's Life: Becoming a Person*. Oxford Universities Press. New York.

TOPIC 1

Playing Is Learning

Playing Is Learning

1. <u>Play is a natural pathway for learning</u>. Throughout nature babies learn social and survival skills through play. Everything a baby touches, hears, smells or sees triggers a new brain connection. When these experiences are pleasurable and fun, learning will be memorable.

Play makes learning easy because fun motivates us to remain in an activity for a longer time. As adults, when we are playing, we share happy emotions. We seem open and collaborative. Patterns and rules are followed, decisions seem to be made easily. Fun leads us to try new skills, or to practice what we know. Sharing fun often leads to meeting new friends who challenge our skill level and who share our joy in learning. These friendships are often deep and fulfilling relationships, which started with having fun together.

2. <u>Babies begin learning at birth</u>. Their eyes start searching their new world immediately, learning to focus and to understand what they are seeing. By one month of age babies begin to smile when they see a human face. There is recognition which brings pleasure. There is also a recognition of learning, of mastering a skill. It is like an inner voice saying, "I can do this," "This is fun," "I want to do more."

Much of a baby's brain structure develops after birth. With each experience a nerve connection is made and with each reoccurrence the connections become stronger and more permanent within the baby's nervous system. It is like a rope: each experience is a strand of learning which makes the rope stronger. Through play, parents can make repeating experiences interesting and enjoyable.

3. <u>Curiosity triggers learning</u>. It is curiosity that leads to exploration and begins the learning process. Curiosity is another internal voice pushing us to explore new things. This is one reason why humans keep learning and growing mentally throughout a lifetime. By exploring, babies discover new things, meet new people, and learn new skills. It is important that babies be given time to explore. The one-year-old moves quickly from object to object, hardly stopping to focus on any toy or task. "W'zhat?" is often one of baby's first words. By joining this exploration, parents can share and expand their baby's learning. Sharing interest in a flower, a bug, or a book opens wonderful worlds in a baby's mind. Exploration leads to discovery. But, the drive to explore can also lead a baby toward danger. Parents need to plan ahead for what those dangers might be.

<u>Play turns discovery into practice</u>. Through play, babies practice what they have discovered. When they discover something interesting, they try it over and over in many different ways until they understand it and are good at it. This practice helps them feel competent and confident in their new knowledge.

4. <u>Practice leads to Mastery</u>. When babies feel confident in a new skill, they feel in control, they now own the skill, they know that they are competent. For example, a new walker may take one or two wobbly steps, arms outstretched, face furrowed with concentration. "How do I lift one foot and stay upright?" As adults, we rarely think about "how to walk." We are confident of our skill; it is "non-conscious," we own it. When babies master a skill, they will "show it off." Then, they will begin to explore the next new challenge.

5. <u>Mastery leads to Pride</u>. Mastery is a feeling of being in control of your self or your environment. Mastery is also an internal voice of motivation for most adults as well as babies because it is a feeling of power. Mastery allows us to feel that we can influence the world around us and that we can meet the challenges in our lives. This feeling of Mastery brings feelings of pride.

6. <u>Parents can structure successful and safe learning experiences for baby</u>. Parents can create opportunities to play and find places which invite safe, successful exploration. Parents can find interesting tasks and find time to teach them. <u>Parents also regulate behavior through play</u>. Playing sets a structure for parents to teach patterns and define rules and limits. Playfulness, surprise and interest are good tools for diverting baby and changing behavior. Parents who share their baby's interest and their baby's play will strengthen their relationship and awaken a love of learning.

- •Why is play a good thing?
- •Where does play lead us?
- •Why is exploration important?
- •What is the feeling of mastery? When have you felt it?
- •How can a parent help make play lead to learning?

Playing Is Learning

Outcomes:

1. Parents will understand why play is important to babies.
2. Parents will comprehend how mastery motivates a baby to learn.
3. Parents will recognize how to structure safe and successful play for babies.
4. Parents will learn and practice how to regulate behavior through play.

Content and Concepts	Instructional Strategies for Parent Groups
INTRODUCTION:	Display Instructor's Building Block #1 (see pg. 1)
❖Play is a natural pathway for learning.	
•When we are having fun, we try new things; we make new friends.	Brainstorm: "What Is Play?"
•Every new experience is a learning activity.	◆Can also use Discussion Questions - "Before Viewing Video."
KEY CONCEPTS:	
❖Babies begin learning at birth—	Ask Parents:
•through new experiences,	-What is a newborn learning?
•through new relationships.	-How does this happen?
	-Is this fun for a baby?
	◆Show PIPE video: Playing Is Learning, section 1 only.
❖Babies learn through play.	◆Handout: "Play Is a Pathway to Learning." Curiosity triggers learning.
•Babies develop feelings of Mastery and Pride.	◆To illustrate, use "W'zhat?" activity.
	◆Review transparency: "The Mastery Cycle."
	◆Discuss: "Mastery." Show the rest of PIPE video: Playing Is Learning, using Video Discussion Guide.

Instructional Strategies for Home Visitors

Terms to Understand

Competent
Good at; capable

◆Discuss with caregiver his/her experiences with play. Brainstorm "What Is Play?"

Confident
Sure of oneself

◆Show PIPE video Playing Is Learning. Before using video, use Video Discussion Guide questions.

Curiosity
Desire to learn or know

Exploration
To examine closely; to range around looking for something new

Ask Parents:
  -What is a newborn learning?
  -How does this happen?
  -Is your baby learning from play?

Independent
Not requiring the direction or help of others; free from control or restriction

To illustrate learning through play, try a ◆"W'zhat?" activity. Discuss how curiosity triggers learning. Share ◆"Play Is a Pathway to Learning."

◆Review chart: "The Mastery Cycle" and discuss ◆"Mastery."

Mastery
Becoming good at something; acquiring a skill

Content and Concepts	Instructional Strategies for Parent Groups

❖ Parents can structure successful learning and safe play for babies.
 	
  • It's important to make time to play with your baby.
 	
  • Play environments should be safe and invite exploration.
 	
  • The "Blocks of Pride" is a technique to help babies learn and make play successful.
	<u>Discuss</u> times and activities which can invite play.
	
	◆ <u>Read and Discuss</u>: "A Good Place to Play." Each parent diagrams a safe play area or room for his/her own baby to explore, using ◆ "Play Time" worksheet.
	
	◆ Handout: "Blocks of Pride." <u>Discuss</u> how using this technique helps babies learn to feel mastery and pride.

❖ Parents can regulate behavior through play.
  • Play can divert or re-direct the baby.
  • Play can expand and re-focus the baby.
  • Play sets rules, like turn-taking.
	<u>Brainstorm</u>:
	
	1) ways to divert a baby through play — with surprise, interest, or excitement,
	2) ways to change what a baby is learning during play,
	3) ways to set limits through play.

<u>**Demonstration:**</u>
◆ **Demonstrate "Blocks of Pride" procedure while playing spontaneously with a baby. This technique will be used in all interactive sessions.**

Evaluation/Closure

◆ Parents complete "I-Can" statements. *or* an "I Can" Box to use in play with child. (see instructions on right)	**Create an "I Can" Box—** ◆ Parents select six statements from the "I-Can" Handout and decorate each side of a small box to illustrate six different ways to provide a successful play experience for baby. Create ways to play with baby using box (e.g. a mobile, put items *in and out*, make a "home" for a stuffed toy from the box, etc.)

Instructional Strategies for Home Visitors

Terms to Understand, cont.

◆ Ask parent to read "A Good Place to Play."

Help parent plan and actualize one of these areas. Assist parent in selecting a safe play area in one or more rooms. Can use ◆"Play Time" worksheet.

◆ Discuss "Blocks of Pride" technique using handout as a guide.

Brainstorm with parent:

1) ways to divert a baby through play — with surprise, interest, or excitement,
2) ways to change what a baby is learning during play,
3) ways to set limits through play.

Motivation
A voice inside urging you on; inner drive

Practice
To repeat; perform frequently

Regulation
Adjust; balance; fine tune

MATERIALS, SUPPLIES, & RESOURCES:

• PIPE Video and Discussion Guide: Playing Is Learning

• Video camera, television and VCR

• Empty box and craft supplies to decorate box

• Notebook for each parent's portfolio

INTERACTIVE SESSION

Activity: Parents practice the "Blocks of Pride" interactive process which will be incorporated into each session. The goal of this activity is to help parents experience each step of a technique which leads baby and parent to feelings of pride.

Hints for Success

Focus on learning the interactive session's process. This is a supervised experiential learning lab.

Focus parent on watching the baby. Teacher becomes the voice of the baby to illustrate the lesson. Help parents experience positive results.

Video tape sessions if possible.

Set the Stage:

1. Explain: Each topic will include an interactive session. Parents will practice activities related to the topic with their babies.

2. Review: "Interactive Session-Time Schedule" and basic procedure (see PIPE Training Manual).

3. ◆Review "Blocks of Pride" procedure. Explain how this will form the framework for all interactive sessions.

Supervised Interaction in Home Visits or in Parent Groups:

☆Parents spontaneously play with their babies while practicing the Blocks of Pride technique. When baby signals disinterest, over-stimulation, or distress, parent changes or stops activity.

Directions/Procedure for Every Interactive Session:

1. Parent prepares a private, quiet area, selects materials or toys appropriate to baby for this activity.
2. Parent gets baby and interacts with baby practicing the activity. (If baby is sleeping, watch others instead.)
3. After session, parent puts materials away, letting baby help if possible.
4. Parent returns baby to nursery or other safe place.
5. Parent completes ◆"Topic Activity Sheet" (see appendix).

Closure:

Review with each parent the videotaped session. What did they enjoy?
What do they think their babies enjoyed? Parent completes ◆"What I Learned."

Expansion/Enrichment:

Parent keeps a log of times he/she plays with the baby. Identify the activity and the things baby learned. Analyze in terms of the ◆"Mastery" flow chart.

══ TOPIC ENHANCERS ══

TOPIC:
Playing Is Learning

For a Parent Group

1. Play Portfolio or Parent's Log—This is a theme or 3-ring notebook which includes selected activities, information sheets, and handouts which the parent will need for each topic. This portfolio helps organize the topics within the Play Unit. As dividers for topics, parents can use copies of the front sheet from each topic.

Parents can also add to this their personal logs. Each parent may write in the log about experiences he or she has with the baby or about feelings experienced as a parent.

2. Bulletin Board: Still pictures of parents and babies playing in nursery.

3. Child care providers model "Blocks of Pride" in nursery.

4. ◆"Blocks of Pride" posted in nursery.

For Parents at Home

•Parent's Log — (see above, Play Portfolio)

•Introduce a new game, toy or play activity to baby using the "Blocks of Pride" technique.

•Make a safe place in the home where parent or caregiver and baby can play.

•Introduce Baby to any activity described in the Playing Is Learning: Video Discussion Guide.

• Babies' natural inclination to explore and master leads them to do things their parents may not like. Using ◆"DOOZYS" (Appendix), discuss with parents and other caregivers ways to manage these behaviors.

What Is Play?

How do you feel when you are playing?

What game or activity makes you feel this way?

Have you learned or improved while playing it?

Have you made friends through a fun activity?

Discussion Questions to Use
<u>Before</u> Viewing the Videotape
<u>Playing Is Learning</u>

1. What have you done for fun that taught you something at the same time? How have other people helped to make learning successful for you?

2. How long do you have to practice something before you are really good at it? How does this apply to children?

3. Every new experience is learning. What does this mean for parents and caregivers of infants?

4. Think of something you have learned that you feel confident about doing. Did you gain this confidence by being watched over, or by learning it on your own? What implication does this have for babies and caregivers?

** This video is designed for you to stop at various points and immediately discuss what you see. Watch for the fades to black and the words of the song to appear. Then pause the tape for discussion.

This video is suitable for
   ♦ giving an overview of the concepts
   ♦ illustrating parent/infant interaction, both good and bad
   ♦ demonstrating parenting techniques.

Notes from video on Discussion Questions can be included in parent's log.

Play Is a Pathway for Learning

Play is a natural pathway for learning.

> Throughout nature babies play. Play is a spontaneous activity which begins in infancy. It is the natural way all babies, animals and humans learn social and survival skills.

Play makes learning easy.

> Babies enjoy pleasurable experiences. They continue doing what makes them happy. They also have fun exploring and trying new things. It is the happy emotions that push or motivate babies to try new things and practice others.

Play leads to many different experiences.

> Everything a baby touches, hears, smells or sees triggers new brain connections. With each pleasurable experience, learning moves forward because babies are challenged by their success. They want to know more and get better.

Play is a time when people cooperate and collaborate.

> During a game or a happy time together, people share easily. Communication flows, rules are followed, decisions are made easily. Sharing fun often leads to meeting new friends who challenge us and increase our learning. Play is not just for babies. When babies share fun with parents, their world expands. They learn to communicate and cooperate. They learn to make friends.

Play makes learning exciting.

> When babies continue to learn through play, they often develop a love for learning. They become motivated to master skills and gain new knowledge because this represents intrigue and fun, as well as power. Play starts the pathway to knowledge, skill, confidence and social acceptance.

"W'zhat?" — Curiosity Games

Activity #1 This activity is a guessing game.
It is designed to build curiosity.
The teacher thinks of an object
that has to do with babies (e.g. toy, cradle).

•The teacher first tells the parents that the object is animal, vegetable, or mineral.

•Students may only ask 20 questions -- which may only be answered by 'yes' or 'no.'

•The teacher may *only* tell whether it is smaller or bigger than some familiar item
in a nursery or home, etc.

> **Example:**
> **the object is a baby bottle.**
> •**The teacher tells the parents the object is *smaller* than a crib
> and is in the category *mineral*.**
> •**Now the parents may ask 20 questions to figure out what the object is.**

When finished, ask parents what made them interested in knowing what the object was.
(Hopefully they will say curiosity.)
How did this lead to learning? (... by exploring or asking questions)

— — — — — — — — — — — — — — **OR** — — — — — — — — — — — — — — —

Activity #2 The teacher displays one or more objects that the parents probably have not
seen before. Use objects that will elicit curiosity:
•an antique item   •a kitchen gadget   •sewing gadget   •carpenter's tool

"W'zhat?" she asks, pretending to be a toddler. Then the teacher asks parents to examine
objects and try to figure out what they are for.

This can be set up in teams and even used as a "timed" competition. As each team
examines and discusses their object, the rest of class watches and answers these questions.

    1. What questions did the parents ask?
    2. Did they try the gadget in different ways?
    3. Were they curious?
    4. Did they learn anything?

The instructor then tells parents about the gadgets.

"W'zhat?"

How did they feel once they knew the answer?

THE MASTERY CYCLE

An internal feeling of control and confidence
A motivation which drives learning

CURIOSITY— EXPLORATION
"What's in there?" "What is it?" "How does it work?"

DISCOVERY—CHALLENGE

"Let's see if I can do it."

LEARNING

"I'll find help ... a model ... a coach."

PRACTICE

"Over and over and over again."

COMPETENCE/MASTERY

"I've got it!" "I'm in control." "I'm good at it."

CONFIDENCE

"I can join the team, get the job."

PRIDE

"I'm OK"   "I like me"   "I'm worthy."

MASTERY & PRIDE

<u>Mastery is feeling in control of yourself or your environment</u>.
Mastery involves learning a new skill, training a muscle, expanding a brain connection. It is about becoming good at something. Once we master a task, we own it. It belongs to us; we can use it at will.

<u>Mastery gives us a sense of power and confidence</u>.
This feeling urges us forward to find something new to learn and to master. We look for the next challenge in order to have that powerful, pride-filled feeling again.

<u>Mastery is an inborn motivator</u>.
This means that it is like a voice inside our heads that urges us on for a lifetime of learning, of meeting challenges, and feeling pride.

THE MASTERY CYCLE

❖ **<u>Curiosity begins the mastery cycle</u>.** Babies are naturally curious. Their eyes are exploring from the minute they are born, wondering, "what's out there, where am I?" The urge to explore is so strong for toddlers that they forget all else. They wander away, walk off of stairs, forget about rules, refuse food — just to satisfy their curiosity. **<u>Curiosity is a gateway to learning</u>.**

❖ **<u>Curiosity leads to exploration</u>.** As babies explore, they discover new things. "What did I find?...How does it work?" **<u>Exploration is what triggers learning</u>.**

❖ **<u>Exploration leads to discovery</u>.** Discovery is exciting. For humans, new things seem challenging. "Can I do this? Can I have that? Can I understand what this is about?" This challenge to try something new pushes us ... to climb mountains, to like using the computer, or even to go to the moon. **<u>Discovery starts the challenge of learning</u>.**

♣ **Learning happens with experimentation.** When babies discover something, they try it many different ways. They look it over, they shake it, they taste it, they pound it, they throw it. If they learn that it tastes good, it is something to eat. If they can not figure out how to understand their discovery, they will ask for your help.

♣ **Learning happens through relationships with other people.** Asking questions, asking for help, watching and modeling are key ways we all learn about something new. Other persons are often the best resource to help us because they can demonstrate and explain. Adults also read for information or instruction in order to understand what they are curious about.

♣ **Practice usually happens after learning begins.** Learning excites a baby; then baby repeats the action, and learning is strengthened. Most toddlers will practice a newly learned skill until they feel in charge of it. The new walker wants to do nothing but practice walking. Walking for an adult does not take thought because the mental pathways are <u>so</u> strong. We have practiced it well. **Practice leads to Competence.**

♣ **Mastery comes with a feeling of Competence.** When beginning walkers feel safe walking with hands outstretched, they try walking while carrying something. They practice and fall; they practice some more until they are good at it. **They feel a sense of control which is the feeling of Mastery.**

♣ **Confidence is that feeling of mastery.** When we feel competent or good at something, we own the new skill. It becomes part of us and we can use this knowledge selectively when we want or need it. We do not have to practice; we know we can walk when we want to. When babies feel confident in their ability to walk, they quit practicing walking and start trying to climb or run instead.

♣ **Pride comes from mastery.** This is what leads to self esteem. When babies know that they can explore, take the challenge, ask questions, practice a new skill, and become competent, they become strong from within. **When you master a skill, you become a new person.**

Part I	Playing is learning, learning is fun.
Part II	A feeling of mastery ... a feeling of might.
Part III	Fun keeps you going, to repeat what you've done.
Part IV	Learning a new thing and getting it right.
Part V	Learning a new thing you've not tried before.
Part VI	Practice and practice till you're satisfied.
Part VII	Playing is learning, not silly and wild. So make time for fun ... Come on, play with your child.

Play Time

Diagram a good place for your baby to play.
Consider and include baby's age, toys or activities, and safety concerns.

A Good Place to Play

Play is important to a baby's growth and development. Babies will play wherever they are. They will be exploring all possible spaces, climbing, jumping, opening doors and drawers, touching, tasting, and testing.

Safety. Children need a safe environment to explore. Remember, the drive to explore is so strong that saying "no, no" will not stop most babies. They will crawl off the step, eat the cleaning soap, or pound with the glass knick-knack. As a parent, safety should be your first concern.

Exploration. Play areas should have lots of open space and a free, unconfined feeling. There should be a variety of objects to look at and to use. There should be different kinds of experiences available for the child.

Even the very small baby likes to look around at many different things and experience different places and different positions. Small babies are exploring and learning with their eyes. They love shadows on the wall, pictures hanging within their sight and—of course—a human face.

At Baby's level. Arrange play areas so that toys are within a baby's reach. Mirrors and pictures should be at baby's eye level. Have a variety of toys that are age-appropriate so that the baby can choose between books, stuffed animals, balls, banging toys, pretend toys, and problem solving toys. Babies will move quickly between these toys and then choose one to focus on.

Change toys often. Have no more than 10 toys out at one time. Every few days, while baby is sleeping, change some of the toys on the toy shelf. This way the selection is always new and interesting to explore and your baby continues to learn from new experiences.

Always remember to keep some favorites available. Babies often love to see a very old toy. A toy that is below their developmental level is comfortable to return to and play with again. Often, as babies develop, they learn to play with an old toy in a new way. This broadens their experience.

Keep special toys in special places. Babies quickly develop patterns of play. They expect certain things to happen with certain toys. Bath toys should be kept with the bath tub. Music box and good night books read only at bedtime. Have car toys for the car seat and changing table toys for diaper changes. This helps these special toys stay appealing and interesting. It also cues baby for appropriate behaviors around these activities.

Join Baby in play. You are your baby's favorite playmate. Human sharing, especially with parents, takes preference over all toys. When you join baby at his or her game, when you imitate baby, when you take turns or become part of a 'pretend,' baby is learning the most.

Words to opening song:

PLAYING IS LEARNING

Playing is learning ... learning is fun.
Fun keeps you going ... to repeat what you've done.
Play leads to new things ... you've not tried before.

You practice and practice ... 'til you're satisfied.
Learning a new thing ... getting it right.
Is a feeling of mastery ... a feeling of might.

Playing is learning ... not silly ... not wild.
So make time for fun, Mama ... play with your child.

BLOCKS OF PRIDE
Learning By *Doing* Is the Best Way to Learn

5. WAIT FOR CHILD TO SHOW PRIDE
Let child bring activity to a close.
If child masters a task, wait for child to look at you.
Congratulate child with love and joy.
Let child choose new activity or repeat this one.
Stop if you know child is tired or hungry.

4. EXTEND AND EXPAND THE PLAY(challenge)
Take turns, imitate the child.
Let child problem solve. Help when frustrated or stuck.
Encourage child with each step of task - "that's good, good job."
Change play slightly or add something new.
Don't correct or scold, ignore mistakes.

3. FOLLOW CHILD'S LEAD (explore)
Let child respond to toys their way.
Follow child's lead.
Continue what child seems to enjoy.
Share interest, excitement and joy.

2. GET CHILD'S ATTENTION
Move close to the child.
Establish eye contact.
Introduce toys or activity.
Start or model play.

1. APPROACH

Assess the child's mood and attention span.
Select appropriate toys or activities.

"I Can"
Help My Baby Learn
Through Play

Answer the following **I Can** questions:

1. I can foster my baby's curiosity by ...

2. I can help my baby communicate during play by ...

3. I can create a safe play environment for my baby by ...

4. I can make time to play with my baby when ...

5. I can help my baby develop independence during play by ...

6. I can help my baby socially during play by ...

7. I can help my baby feel a sense of mastery and pride during play by ...

What I Learned

1. What is play?

2. How does play provide learning for your baby?

3. How does mastery motivate a baby to learn?

4. Why is playing with your baby important to you?

5. What kinds of activities or play do you like to do with your baby?

6. What are ways a parent can provide successful, safe play areas?

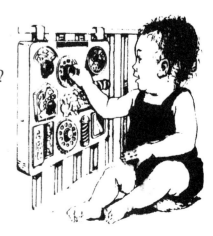

Playing Is Learning About Differences

Playing Is Learning About Differences

1. <u>Play is a way to learn about differences</u>. Play defines differences in babies. During the first three years of life a baby's ability to learn and play changes almost every month. Their brains and bodies are developing quickly. It is through observing and participating in play that parents can stay in tune with their baby's development. Along with the changes in maturation, there are differences in babies due to inborn characteristics like genetics and temperament. Each baby is learning in very different ways and at very different rates. Play is a good way to see the individual in each baby.

2. <u>Emotional needs are the core or center for all babies' learning</u>. Emotion is the language of infancy. Babies are born able to understand and communicate through emotional signals. It is through this emotional connection that babies feel safe and protected. Through sharing the positive emotions of their parents, babies feel the balance or equilibrium which is needed for strong development. This sense of closeness or attachment to parents forms the foundation for subsequent learning and development.

Because babies' emotional needs are developing along with their physical changes, the first three years are a constant seesaw in the relationship with parents. Infants are totally dependent on their caregivers for survival and protection. But, when babies have mastered some developmental skills, they celebrate by showing independence. They often become demanding and seem focused outward. As babies begin to learn a new developmental skill—like crawling—this independence changes. They become cautious, whining, and clinging. They seem shy, hide their heads and copy whatever their parents are doing. These developmental transition periods in the emotional needs of the baby are as important as physical development. Understanding when babies need to be close and when babies need autonomy helps to avoid a mismatch in relationship which can disorganize development and learning.

3. <u>Understanding a baby's development helps facilitate learning</u>. When the baby was in the womb, mother's body provided just the right environment for the baby to grow from embryo to infant. After birth, parents still provide the best environment for development. Parents set the stage, find the toys, assess baby's mood, and decide what to reinforce or ignore. In order to do this, parents need to be able to understand what their baby is able to do and what their baby will be able to learn next. Then parents can change their expectations and their behavior to stay "in tune" with the baby's learning level. They will not expect too much or become cross with baby's mistakes.

4. <u>As babies develop, learning changes</u>. Growth and maturation provide a natural cycle for mastery. When babies begin to stretch their hands and feet outward, their parents provide something close and safe to touch, like a mobile. The baby touches the mobile and the figures move. This brings pleasure and baby tries reaching again. A new game is made. Muscles become schooled and toned, a new skill is learned. Baby is now ready for the next developmental step. The mastery cycle can begin anew. This is the way babies continue to learn and to develop. However, with each new skill the baby will be learning in a different way. When reaching is assimilated, grabbing and pulling will be the next learning level. This challenges parents to think ahead about safety. Now the mobile needs to be moved up so baby won't grab and eat it. Now a different kind of toy can be added to the baby's world.

5. <u>There is a readiness factor to learning</u>. As muscle strength and size change, a baby's ability to perform new skills changes. If babies are not developmentally ready for a new task, they will reject it. When babies refuse to play, ask why? Are they developmentally ready? This means respecting babies when they refuse a new toy or activity. Return to an old favorite that represents success. Emotionally supportive communications are keys to fostering babies who will learn and advance easily.

Variety provides balance in development. When parents provide many different play experiences like finger food or finger paint, jumping or sliding activities, quiet singing or reading activities, each experience adds new connections in the baby's brain. Readiness to learn more is enriched.

5. <u>Play is influenced by temperament</u>. Temperament refers to the way we react or respond to the world around us. We usually express temperament through emotional signals. These signals help us and those around us to know how we feel about a situation. (To teach temperament, see Topic 2 in <u>Love Is Layers of Sharing</u>.) Much of what parents refer to as temperament will change with each developmental step. As babies' brains mature and as their skills advance, their reactions to people and places will change. Temperament is also strongly influenced by babies' relationships with their parents. The way parents share emotions and experiences can modify temperament during the early years.

6. <u>When parents are emotionally "in tune," parenting is fun</u>. This will happen if parents understand their babies' developmental level and how babies' temperament may impact this. When parents share play activities with their babies, they will provide equilibrium. When parent and baby change together, it is like an orchestra — they make beautiful music because they are "in tune."

> •How can parents stay "in tune" with their babies?
> •What does the readiness factor mean to learning?
> •How does temperament influence play?
> •What are the developmental stages?
> •What does developmentally appropriate play mean?
> •How does appropriate play unlock learning?

Playing Is Learning About Differences

Outcomes:

1. Parents will become aware of a baby's stages of development and unique temperament.
2. Parents will understand there is a readiness factor to learning.
3. Parents will select and practice developmentally appropriate play activities with their babies.
4. Parents can explain ways to help baby find emotional balance.

Content and Concepts	Instructional Strategies for Parent Groups
INTRODUCTION: ❖ It is through play that parents can stay "in tune" with their baby's development. •Play is a way to learn about differences. •Play is a way to see the individual in baby. •Parents need to change with baby to stay "in tune." **KEY CONCEPTS:** ❖ As a baby develops, baby will change. There are many areas of development, which do not all change at once. ❖Play helps parents see babies change. •Readiness to learn is influenced by growth, maturation and emotional security.	Display Instructor's Building Block #2 (see pg. 25) •Use "In Tune" Activity to introduce concept of staying "in tune" with a baby's development. Discuss: -How babies are constantly changing in the first year. -Each developmental step leads to new skills— for both parents and babies. -Learning about development helps parents stay "In Tune." Introduce and explain areas of development. •Handout: "Overview of Developmental Areas." Parents find and share pictures in magazines which illustrate each of the areas. The Magna System Videos provide an in-depth look at each area of development (see resource list). Explain how babies do not learn until they are ready developmentally - what do they do instead? (fuss, refuse, ignore) •Explain and demonstrate "Readiness to Learn." •Define: Developmental Milestones using "What Are Developmental Milestones?" Discuss milestones each baby has recently achieved. What play activities did baby enjoy at each stage? When were these observed?

Instructional Strategies for Home Visitors

Terms to Understand

◆Adapt the "In Tune" Activity by encouraging additional caregivers to join the session. Explore the concept of "staying in tune." If no one else can join, do the activity with caregiver, or do handclapping if no instruments are available.

Discuss: how learning about development helps parents stay "In Tune," how babies are constantly changing in the first year, and how each developmental step leads to new skills for both parents and babies.

Introduce and explain areas of development.
◆Share: "Overview of Developmental Areas." Bring several magazines which have pictures illustrating each of the areas. Share with mom. Use videos from resource list to go in-depth on one or more area(s) of development.

Explain how babies do not learn until they are ready developmentally. What do they do instead? (fuss, refuse, ignore)

Discuss "Readiness to Learn."

◆Discuss handout: "What Are Developmental Milestones?" Focus on the milestones baby has recently achieved. What play activities did baby enjoy at each stage?

Adapt
Adjust or change as the situation changes; to fit in with, or accept new things; to grow and develop

Cognitive
The ability to think and process and understand knowlege

Developmental Milestone
A significant point of change in one's abilities due to maturation

Emotional development
Being able to express and act upon your feelings with balance and self control

Equilibrium
Balance; a mid-point between opposing forces

Fine Motor
Control of small muscles

Content and Concepts	Instructional Strategies for Parent Groups
	◆Show: Sample "Personal Development Profile." Parent develops: "My Baby's Personal Development Profile" (PDP) using a form from a standard developmental test as a guide (see resource list.) Parents identify as many as five emerging milestones in each category— ones that their babies will develop in the next few months.
•Developmentally appropriate play is a key to learning.	Parent identifies types of play, activities or toys which would correspond to the emerging abilities listed on PDP. Select activities from PIPE Cards or have parents make activity cards using other sources (using blank activity card forms).
•As Baby develops, temperament changes. - Baby's temperament influences play and learning.	◆Review: "RYB's View of Temperament" from Love Is Layers of Sharing text, Topic 2. Parent rates baby's temperament using "Temperament Study Sheet." Discuss: -How a baby's temperament changes play time. -How does development change temperament? -How can shared emotions change temperament?
❖Emotional connections are the core for all baby's learning. •Emotion is the language babies use. •Newborns can read emotional signals. •Babies share parents' emotions. •As baby develops emotionally, relationships change. •The first three years are an emotional seesaw.	Discuss: how parent and Baby communicate through emotional signals. ◆Handout transparency: "Emotional Seesaw." Discuss: Dependence versus Independence How can parents stay "In Tune" and provide emotional balance?

Demonstration:

Demonstrate developmentally appropriate vs. developmentally inappropriate activities with a baby. Use Activity Cards "Playing While Learning About Differences" or the cards parents created.

Evaluation/Closure

My baby is like other babies because ...
My baby is different from other babies because ...
Complete ◆"Checking What I Learned" (see Appendix).

Parents answer these open-ended questions. This may be conducted as a verbal round table with the child care supervisor attending to contribute positive observations about these parents' children in the child care setting.

Instructional Strategies for Home Visitors

◆ Show: Sample "Personal Development Profile." Parent develops: "My Baby's Personal Development Profile" (PDP) using a standard developmental form from a standard developmental test (see resource list.)
Parents identify as many as five emerging milestones per category for their own babies.

Help parent to identify developmentally appropriate games for her child using the baby's developmental chart (PDP) as a guide.

◆ Review: "RYB's View of Temperament" from Love Is Layers of Sharing text, Topic 2. Parent rates baby's temperament using "Temperament Study Sheet."

Discuss:
-How a baby's temperament changes play time.
-How does development change temperament?
-How can shared emotions change tempera
ment?

Discuss: how parents and babies communicate through emotional signals.

◆ Use the information sheet "Emotional Seesaw" to discuss the emotional needs for attachment and autonomy. How do parents need to change to keep baby emotionally balanced?

Terms to Understand, cont.

Gross Motor
Control of large muscles

Maturation
To become fully developed or complete; growing and changing toward a desired state of personal acceptance and balance

PDP - Personal Development Profile
A form each parent uses to chart his or her baby's developmental change

Readiness Factor
Being neurologically and emotionally able to learn

Self Care
Being able to meet one's own needs

Social Development
Developmental changes which will help babies connect with others, i.e. smiling, laughing, imitating

MATERIALS, SUPPLIES, & RESOURCES:

• Parent and baby magazines (scissors are optional in activity)
• Any kind of musical instruments, such as: kazoos, xylophones, spoons, whistles, drums, bells, etc.
• Camera, nursery song tape, tape recorder
• A simple pegboard toy, or cardboard box and 6 dowels
• See resources list: Developmental Tests such as Denver II, HELP, KID, CDI, "Ages and Stages"
• Learning Games for First Three Years

INTERACTIVE SESSION

Activity: Parents practice Developmentally Appropriate Play using PIPE Activity Cards or activities selected by each parent, based on the baby's PDP. The goal of this activity is for parents to experience how some activities "fit" their child better than others.

Hints for Success

Spend time helping each parent identify techniques that will be successful with his/her baby.

If feasible, have all parents do same activities with their babies.

Monitor techniques and interaction closely.

Videotape the session.

Set the Stage:

1. Review the stages of development.

2. Demonstrate what happens when a baby is playing something which is inappropriate for his/her age.

3. Review temperament worksheet. How will baby's present temperament affect play?

4. Re-emphasize that when you and your baby are "in tune," it is like an orchestra playing music.

Supervised Interaction in Home Visits or in Parent Groups:

☆ 1. Practice an activity that is developmentally appropriate. Then pick one that is not a developmental fit and see the contrast in the baby's response. [Use an activity that is likely to be a poor fit as well as one that is a good fit so parent can see contrast in baby's responses.]

2. See directions and procedures in Introduction (page vii).

Closure:

Review with each parent the videotaped session. Discuss how play is enhanced when baby's development and temperament are understood.

Parents make a list of age-appropriate activities they each can do with Baby.

Expansion/Enrichment:

Parents periodically check the baby's development using baby's individual PDP.

Parents review and recheck baby's temperament chart. Were there changes?

TOPIC:
Playing Is Learning About Differences

For a Parent Group

1. Parents may keep in their portfolios ongoing personal development profiles and temperament charts throughout the year. Were there changes? Why?

2. ◆Post "Blocks of Pride." Discuss how these steps might change with development.

3. Bulletin Board: Illustrate developmental milestones—use pictures of babies in nursery if possible, or pictures parents found in magazines at home or during instructional session.

4. Invite the Child Find Coordinator or other child development specialist as guest speaker.

5. Have a "Child Fair," each parent bringing an age-appropriate activity for his or her baby. Discuss three ways to use each activity so that parent and baby are both interested.

6. Make toys or plan activities which are age-appropriate for baby.

For Parents at Home

•In portfolio, each parent keeps an ongoing list of interactive activities which are age-appropriate for his or her baby.

•Make a "wish list" of age-appropriate activities and toys for baby's ongoing development. Explain to family and friends why these activities/toys are appropriate.

• Babies' changing abilities lead them to do things their parents may not like. Using ◆"DOOZYS" (Appendix), discuss with parents and other caregivers ways to manage these behaviors.

=== "In Tune" Activity ===

Instructions:

•Using different musical instruments (e.g. kazoos), the parents try to play a nursery song together, i.e. "Ring-Around-the-Rosie," or "Twinkle, Twinkle, Little Star," etc.

•Play the song slowly; then try playing it faster. Then try once more, with everyone staying together. Hand clapping can be used if instruments are not available.

Discuss:

•Did some know the song better than others?

•Did some know more about playing the instruments than others?

•Could they tell who knew more when they played together?

•Did they have fun even though the song wasn't completely polished?

•What would it be like if everyone knew how to play that tune?

Evaluate:

•How each person might be at a different skill level.

•The people who knew more about the song or instrument had to wait and be patient with those who were learning.

•They had to change the way they might play in order to be "in tune" with the group. They had to match their ability to the group.

•Babies will be changing their abilities constantly as they develop.

•Each developmental step leads to new skills. The experience they have with each new skill leads to learning and knowledge. It will be like first playing a new tune.

•Babies can become frustrated. Parent and baby can become "out of tune."

Now, play a taped nursery song:

•How does it sound? Is it better than the parents' song? What might baby like best? Why?

Discuss:

How learning about child development will alert parents to what may change in their babies. Why is knowing about development a good way to see the baby as an individual? How does playing together alert parents to developmental changes?

> **Parents who understand about infant development can adapt to the learning level of their babies. They can have fun playing, and they can stay "in tune."**

Overview of Developmental Areas

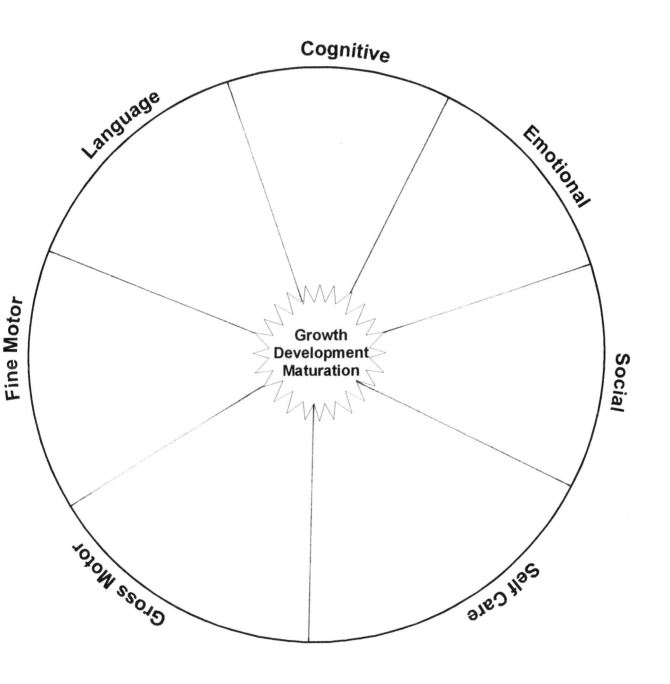

Readiness to Learn

Babies cannot learn some things until their brains are ready. That is, certain neurological connections must be made before a baby can do a task or solve a problem. Their parents must be patient and wait until a baby is developmentally ready for certain behaviors or tasks. When they are not ready, they will turn away, ignore, or fuss about the task.

Parents can see their babies change developmentally through play.
Here are some developmental games.

1-4 month old baby
Mouthing Games

Open and close your mouth, or make puckering, kissing movements with your mouth. Do this several times, and then wait and watch. Your baby will begin to copy you. As your baby develops, his or her mouthing movements will become more distinct and more like yours. You can begin to take turns. Also, change something by sticking out your tongue or smacking your lips. **Baby will be ready to take a further developmental step by 4 months.**

5-8 month old baby
Play Peek-a-Boo Game

Use a small cloth or cardboard. Cover your face.Then pull it away and smile. Say "Hi, Baby." (<u>Not</u> Boo!) Repeat several times. Wait for baby's response.

As baby develops, you can pull cloth away slowly, showing your face a little at a time. Baby will recognize you and laugh.

By 8 months, you can cover the baby's face with the small cloth and then pull it off saying "Where's baby?" After a few tries, wait for baby to pull the cloth off and laugh. (If baby seems frightened, change the game back to covering your face.) Let the baby pull the cloth away from her face. A baby this young is not developmentally ready to be in the dark under the cloth.

Do not use large blankets or dish towels. Baby can get tangled up in them and become afraid. Watch your baby's expression. Baby's face will tell you about his or her developmental readiness.

Teasing a baby is very detrimental. If a baby is not developmentally ready, the joke you think you are playing will be "lost" on Baby.

-continued

Playing Is Learning

9-24 month old baby
Peg Board Game

Using a cardboard box top and 6 large dowels, make holes in the box top and stand dowels upright in the holes. This makes a peg board which will be a fun learning experience for babies who are advancing their thinking skills.

9 Months:
Baby likes to handle the pegs. Baby will play with one dowel in many ways. Baby likes to feel it, turn it over, bang with it, and chew it.

12 Months:
Stand one dowel up through hole in the box top and give top to the baby. Baby will take dowel out, examine it, taste it and try to put it into a hole in the box. If baby succeeds, this will become an interesting and repeated task. Give baby a second dowel and see what happens. Is baby developmentally ready?

15 Months:
Give baby all the dowels and the box top with one dowel standing up. Baby will take dowel out and then return it. Then baby will try to put the other dowels in other holes. Baby may need your help. Baby may get tired and not finish or want to put all of the dowels in the same hole. This will show you baby's developmental stage. Don't expect too much, too soon.

20 Months:
Give baby all the dowels standing in the box top. Take dowels out and give them to the baby. Baby will stand all dowels up in their holes, and then take them out and do it again and look to you for approval. Some babies become very fast. They enjoy the mastery of their skill at this developmental stage.

24 Months:
The baby may ignore the dowel task all together or put it aside or throw it. Why do you think this is the case?

A Progression of Transitions
Developmental Steps

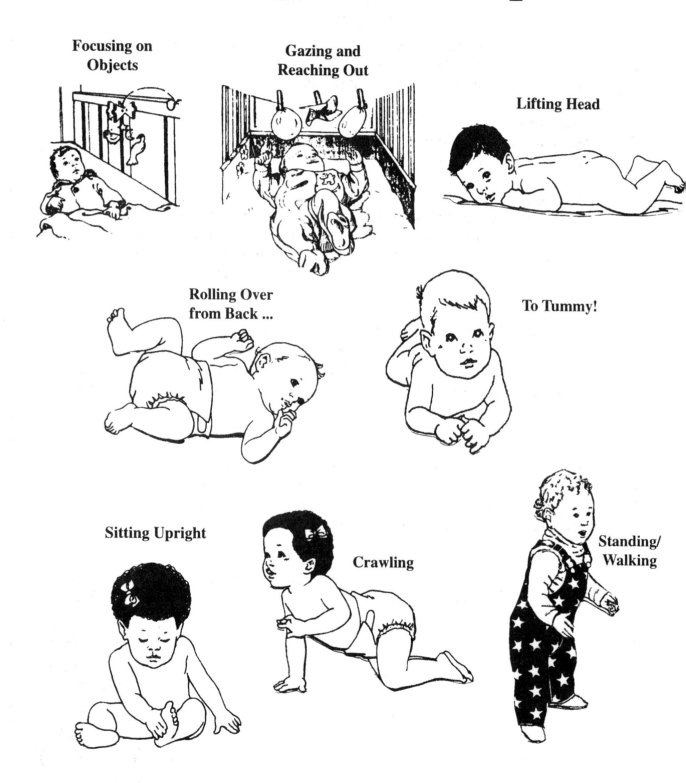

Focusing on Objects

Gazing and Reaching Out

Lifting Head

Rolling Over from Back ...

To Tummy!

Sitting Upright

Crawling

Standing/ Walking

Playing Is Learning

My Baby's Personal Development Profile (PDP)

Baby's Name _Jane Doe_   Birthdate _Oct. 5, 1986_

Use a standard developmental assessment to list below developmental milestones that your baby has just gained. <u>At the left side of this page</u>, record one milestone for <u>each</u> developmental area. Next to each milestone, put your baby's age <u>in the Evaluation Box, column #1</u>.

Return to the standard developmental form and for each area select 3 more milestones *that you believe your baby will develop in the next four months*. Save item #5 for an unexpected milestone. Check next month and record under the Evaluation Box, column #2 the age at which baby developed the next milestone. Then the next month, record in Evaluation Box, column #3. This will create a Personal Development Profile (PDP) for you and your baby. This chart can be extended for up to three years.

MY BABY'S PHYSICAL SKILLS

GROSS MOTOR

1. Holds head upright
2. Stiffens, pushes with feet
3. Lifts head when on tummy
4. Rolls over
5.

When Did Development Occur? — Age

2 mo.			

FINE MOTOR

1. Relaxes fingers, open hands
2. Reaches for objects
3. Grasps a dangling object
4. Holds a rattle
5.

When Did Development Occur? — Age

2 mo.			

MY BABY'S SOCIAL/EMOTIONAL SKILLS

1. Smiles at caregivers
2. Quiets when picked up
3. Reaches for caregiver
4. Seems aware of strangers
5.

When Did Development Occur? — Age

2 mo.			

<u>Sample:</u> My Baby's Personal Development Profile, cont.

MY BABY'S COGNITIVE SKILLS

1. Turns eyes toward sound
2. Smiles at caregivers
3. Quiets when talked to
4. Purposeful reaching
5.

When Did Development Occur? — Age

2 mo.			

MY BABY'S LANGUAGE SKILLS

1. Has many different sounds
2. Imitates cooing sounds
3. Laughs outloud
4. Practices different sounds
5.

When Did Development Occur? — Age

2 mo.			

MY BABY'S SELF CARE SKILLS

1. Sucks well from breast or bottle
2. Is able to quiet self for sleep
3. Has a predictable schedule
4. Wants to hold own bottle or spoon
5.

When Did Development Occur? — Age

2 mo.			

My Baby's Personal Development Profile (PDP)

Baby's Name_____   Birthdate _____

Use a standard developmental assessment to list below developmental milestones that your baby has just gained. At the left side of this page, record one milestone for each developmental area. Next to each milestone, put your baby's age in the Evaluation Box, column #1.

Return to the standard developmental form and for each area select 3 more milestones *that you believe your baby will develop in the next four months.* Save item #5 for an unexpected milestone. Check next month and record under the Evaluation Box, column #2 the age at which baby developed the next milestone. Then the next month, record in Evaluation Box, column #3. This will create a Personal Development Profile (PDP) for you and your baby. This chart can be extended for up to three years.

MY BABY'S PHYSICAL SKILLS

GROSS MOTOR

When Did Development Occur? — Age

1.

2.

3.

4.

5.

FINE MOTOR

When Did Development Occur? — Age

1.

2.

3.

4.

5.

MY BABY'S SOCIAL/EMOTIONAL SKILLS

When Did Development Occur? — Age

1.

2.

3.

4.

5.

My Baby's Personal Development Profile, cont.

MY BABY'S COGNITIVE SKILLS

1.
2.
3.
4.
5.

When Did Development Occur? — Age

MY BABY'S LANGUAGE SKILLS

1.
2.
3.
4.
5.

When Did Development Occur? — Age

MY BABY'S SELF CARE SKILLS

1.
2.
3.
4.
5.

When Did Development Occur? — Age

This chart is a sample of what can be created by a parent. Developmental "checkpoints" can be added as Baby grows. Each parent's list should be adapted to Baby's development. There are also commercial developmental assessments that can be purchased.

Temperament Study Sheet

How would you rate your baby's temperament today? Think about the ways your baby responds to his/her environment. In the spaces below evaluate your baby's temperament. Give examples of some situations where you have observed this about your baby.

1. **ACTIVITY LEVEL** *Some babies are more active, while others sleep, sit or play quietly. Active infants squirm, roll over, or push away. Quiet babies tend to lie where they are placed.*

I think my baby's activity level is:

a. Very active   b. Active   c. Quiet

Example:

2. **PREDICTABILITY** *Some babies seem to have a built in alarm clock. After a few months they eat, nap and have bowel movements at predictable times. Some are simply unpredictable!*

My baby's habits are:

a. Very predictable   b. Fairly predictable   c. Unpredictable

Example:

3. **COMFORT WITH NEW SITUATIONS** *Babies respond differently to new foods, their first bath, new people and new experiences. Some babies adapt easily, while others cling to parents.*

My baby adapts to new situations:

a. With little trouble   b. Fairly easily   c. With difficulty

Example:

4. **SENSITIVITY** *Some babies cry when experiencing noise, light, soiled diapers, changes in temperature, textured clothing, or a new food. Others don't react noticeably to these changes.*

My baby is:

                a. Extremely sensitive   b. Somewhat sensitive

<u>Example</u>:

5. **THINKER-or-DOER** *Some babies seek out new experiences and toys and like to discover new things. Others stay close, need support to approach something new.*

My baby:

      a. Is an explorer   b. Sometimes starts to explore by him/herself   c. Needs a pal to get started

<u>Example</u>:

6. **DISTRACTIBILE OR FOCUSED** *Some babies focus on what they are doing regardless of who comes into the room or what else happens. Other babies can easily be distracted. Each change of Mom's attention stops baby's focus.*

My baby is:

      a. Easily distracted   b. Sometimes distracted   c. Never distracted

<u>Example</u>:

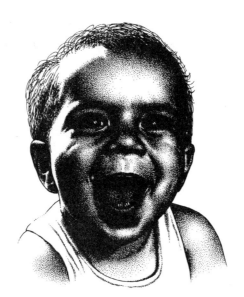

44

The Emotional Seesaw

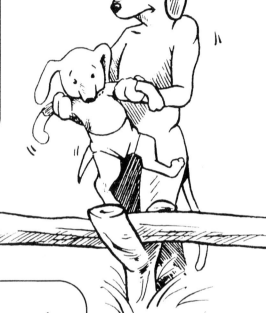

1-3 mos.
Birth to physical equilibrium
Babies are searching for survival and stable patterns for eating and sleeping.

Dependent / Off-Balance
Baby is "one" with Mom. Needs nourishment, protection, close bodily contact. Seeking survival. Requires time and commitment from parents.

4-6 mos.
Early development (purposeful reaching, grabbing, voice sounds, etc.) give baby a sense of power. Babies realize they control their bodies and voices. They realize they influence others.

Independent / In-Balance
Emotional signals expand; laughs, whimpers, grunts, coughs, squeaks, sighs, etc. Baby experiments with response of others. Turns away from Mom. Looks for new things, new people. Goes easily to others. Cries when left alone. Plays easily with Dad and Grandma.

7-10 mos.
Babies move away and into trouble. Crawling begins.

Dependent / Off-Balance
Baby feels unsure, unsafe, needs parents close. Parents become the guide and the model. Baby wants to be held more, seems to be anxious. Watches and copies parents. Fusses at strangers. Needs special cuddly toys, own cup, chair, etc.

The Emotional Seesaw, *cont.*

11-15 mos.
Babies feel powerful. They take initiative
and become demanding. Walking begins.

Independent / In-Balance
*Babies explore, question, test limits. They run away from
parents, want to do things alone, use parents' things, copy
parents, and eat their food. Emotional signals become extreme,
out-of-control. Uncontrolled crying and raucous laughter.*

16-24 mos.
Using words, learning about relationships.
Babies wonder, "Where do I belong?" "How do I act?"

Dependent / Off-Balance
*Babies are learning do's and don'ts and about anger in adults.
They seek closeness to parents, "Are you there?" "Am I safe?"
"Do you like me?" They want to be held often. Question parents.
Ask to learn, "W'zhat?" Prolong bedtime; night waking returns.*

The Emotional Seesaw, *cont.*

25-30 mos.
Ask questions; communicate emotions. Babies begin
to remember, understand, and follow directions.

Independent / Confident,
but ... also Unsure, Off-Balance

*Babies now enjoy other relationships. They use words to state wants.
They feel happy and powerful. They are demanding; they experiment with
emotional extremes. Frustration and tantrums are common. Babies fly
out-of-control and can't get back. They need emotional stability from
their parents. They cling to parents when they leave and keep a memory
object (teddy or blanket) to remind themselves of this emotional base.*

31-36 mos.
Confident and competent little persons. Babies
understand and cooperate, join in, and help out.

In-Balance / Sure

*Babies now feel confident in parents' love and protection.
They keep "teddy" close to feel parental stability. They enjoy
meeting others and being with other children. They negotiate their
needs, understand a plan of action, follow directions. They anticipate household patterns and know the do's and don'ts. They enjoy
their parents and try hard to please. In-balance, toddlers of this
age love making things, doing puzzles, and playing skill games.*

◆ The Emotional Seesaw ◆

Our emotions define our thinking and our actions.

Emotional development is about learning how to manage emotions.
It is about communicating and regulating our emotions successfully.
It is about learning to balance our feelings with the feelings of others.

Emotional balance happens because of relationships with other humans.

It is through relationships that our human needs are met.
It is because of relationships that we feel pride or shame.
It is because of relationships that we learn to "fit in," to belong.
It is because of relationships that we feel safe and accepted.

The first three years—for a baby—are an emotional seesaw.

There are periods of mastery, "I can do it!"
There are periods of insecurity. "This is new, strange...I need help!"
Emotions swing wildly out of control.

The seesaw moves between feeling off-balance and in-balance.

Babies feel off-balance because they are constantly changing,
physically and mentally. They feel dependent,
needing a protector, a model, a guide.

Babies feel in-balance when they gain a skill or learn a pattern.
They feel confident. They feel independent,
"I'm ok, I can do it. I'll try anything!"

In the first three years, babies are learning how to control these feelings.

They are learning how to use emotions to communicate.
They are learning how to regulate extremes of emotion.
They are learning the power of sharing emotion.
Babies need help to find balance.

Parents are baby's first relationship.
Parents provide the stability to steady this seesaw.

For parents, staying "in-tune" is a tricky job!

❖**Babies are born understanding emotional signals.**
   This is how they connect with other humans.
   This is how they find protection and make attachments.

❖**Babies also communicate through emotional signals.**
   They "tune-in" or "tune-out" of the world around them.
   They use their bodies, faces, and voices to show their feelings.

❖**Babies often feel off-balance and unsure.**
   They reach out for help and guidance.
   They attach to a few special persons.

When babies feel off-balance, parents should plan more time to hold them, to protect them and be a guide. Expect less of the baby. Keep routines stable.

When babies feel in-balance, parents should allow baby more autonomy. Let baby show off new skills. Give baby room to explore. Be tolerant. Manage the extremes of emotion with quiet control. These are times to provide new learning experiences. Use this confidence to expand learning.

TOPIC 3

Baby's First Teacher

Baby's First Teacher

1. <u>Babies are born ready to learn from other humans</u>. They respond more often and more positively to human faces, voices and touch than they do to objects, mobiles or bright patterns around them. Babies are motivated to belong and to "fit in" with humankind. This is true for all of us. We strive to please, copy, and belong with other people. *Therefore, in the first three years, most learning is about relationships.* "How do I survive? Where do I belong? How do I behave? How do I get what I want?" These are social skills that are dependent on other humans. Unlike developmental milestones, these skills are learned from parents and from the environment that parents provide.

2. <u>Parents are babies' first teachers</u>. Parents are the first and most consistent human experience in an infant's life. Babies depend on their parents for nutrition, protection, and stimulation. It is a mother, father or other caregiver who first connects the baby to feelings of trust and belonging. Parents or surrogate parents create the context in which babies will experience other humans. Parents show babies how to get along with others. They set the goals and define the limits in their babies' lives. Parents are the models and the mentors. They are the guardians and the coaches. Parents also organize and help strengthen emotional pathways. By the way they respond to their babies' needs, they can help their babies feel positive, valued and competent.

3. <u>Parents are the most powerful teachers for babies</u>. The biological tie between parent and child defines a special emotional tie which will be there for a lifetime. Many other relationships will be wonderful, providing stability and learning experiences for the child, but they are time defined and usually end. It is the parents who wrap their babies in a continuous fabric of protection, shared emotions, stability and learning.

4. <u>Parents need to master skills to become good teachers</u>. During the first year, parents will be using skills of guidance, co-regulation, and shared emotion. They will be learning how to listen to a baby, to provide a supportive framework for a baby's development, to provide feelings of safety and trust. They learn to give simple, clear messages, to use interest words to gain the baby's attention and to be consistent in their messages to their babies. Learning "the teaching loop" provides parents with confidence in their parenting.

5. <u>Every moment with a baby is a teachable moment</u>. Babies are watching, listening, touching and learning about their environment with most every waking moment. They learn the most by sharing emotions with their parents. Dressing, eating, traveling, reading, exercising, quiet times, and good night times—these are all times of emotional sharing with parents. There are times to find fun by exploring sights, sounds, ideas. There are times to share sadness and frustration. There are times to share calm, close, contented feelings. It is through emotions that babies understand their parents and feel connected to them. It is through this emotional connectedness that learning occurs.

6. <u>Routines are a good way to teach</u>. Routines are patterns of behavior which happen often and let babies know what to expect. This pattern gives baby confidence, knowing what will come next. It gives babies a sense of safety and balance. Because of this, routines provide some of the strongest learning experiences. Routines help establish trust and respect in a relationship. Routines give babies physical balance; their bodies know what to expect, and they know when their needs will be met. Routines teach babies to anticipate and to be patient. When they have learned how to join into the routine, they feel mastery.

•Why are parents so important in the learning process?
•How do parents become good teachers?
•What are teachable moments?
•How do routines influence learning?

Baby's First Teacher

Outcomes:

1. Parents will analyze why they are baby's first teacher.
2. Parents will identify teachable moments and what the baby is learning
3. Parents will practice skills for teaching their babies.

Content and Concepts	Instructional Strategies for Parent Groups
INTRODUCTION: ❖Babies are born ready to learn from other humans. •Babies prefer people to things -for example, a face to a rattle. •Babies are learning to cooperate and negotiate by watching others. **KEY CONCEPTS:** ❖Parents are baby's first teacher. •Parents and babies have a biological tie. •Parents are the most constant human experience for a baby. •Parents set patterns for baby's life. By defining recurring events (eating, sleeping, playing) with a regular procedure, parents are setting a familiar pattern, which has shared meaning. These are the first experiences in a baby's memory.	Display Instructor's Building Block #3 (see pg. 51) ◆Use handout: "People Prefer People." Discuss why people prefer humans over things. Show video clip: Love's Labors, which illustrates babies prefer people. Explain why social/emotional development depends on other humans. -They protect us; they are caring. -They provide models and guides. -They help us feel OK, which gives us balance. ◆Brainstorm, using overhead: "Who teaches your baby?" Using individual pictures of each baby and parent, tie a ribbon between them. Why is this time unique? Discuss: 　　1) Who meets baby's needs the most? 　　2) Who will baby trust the most? 　　3) Who will baby watch most? ◆Hand out "Word Scramble" (see instruction sheet). Discuss how a familiar pattern becomes comfortable and meaningful. Patterns provide shared meanings. Shared meaning is key to "fitting in" or belonging with others.

Instructional Strategies for Home Visitors	**Terms to Understand**

◆Discuss handout/activity "People Prefer People." Explain why social/emotional development depends on other humans.
 	
    -They protect us; they are caring.
    -They provide models.
    -They help us feel OK which gives us balance.
Talk about the caregivers and other adults or children who will "teach" baby. What things might baby learn from each one? Why are parents the most important teachers?
	Ambivalent
	Uncertain of how one feels; able to see both sides of an issue.

Ask parents to create a photo page or a refrigerator poster that shows how their baby shares various traits with their parents. Highlight physical and temperamental similarities.	**Dyad** A pair; a relationship between two people **Empathy** The capacity for sharing in the interests and feelings of another
	Guidance Direction and support from another

Discuss with Parent:
  -Who meets baby's needs the most?
  -Who sets baby's daily patterns and routines?
	Mentor
	A trusted counselor or guide

◆Share "Word Scramble." How do patterns lead to shared meaning, shared understanding and trust?	**Modeling** Acting as a model or pattern for baby to copy

Content and Concepts	Instructional Strategies for Parent Groups
❖Every moment with a baby is a Teachable Moment. •Daily routines are times of sharing. •Sharing fun is a pathway to learning. •Playing during caretaking routines gives parents a way to focus baby.	◆Handout: "Teachable Moments." Discuss how regular caretaking events can become moments of shared meaning. Sharing interest and fun increases learning. ◆ Parents complete "Teachable Moments With My Baby."
❖Establishing daily routines helps learning. •Routines set shared expectations. -Knowing what will happen next gives a sense of safety. -This gives baby balance and trust. - From within these routines, learning can expand.	Brainstorm: How do routines create patterns for baby? -Why do patterns give feelings of safety & confidence? -What do babies learn from patterns? ◆Review information sheet: "Routines Become Teachable Moments." Use other references which include steps and routines. See The Developing Child. ◆Complete "Family Routines Worksheet."
❖There are skills for becoming a good teacher.	◆Using overheads, illustrate "The Teaching Loop." This is a way to initiate learning.

Demonstration:

Demonstrate a teachable moment during a diapering demonstration, following the steps in the teaching loop.

Evaluation/Closure

◆Complete "I AM" form.

◆Each parent creates a classified ad.

To create a "classified ad," detail the job description and describe the ideal candidate for your Baby's First Teacher.

Instructional Strategies for Home Visitors	**Terms to Understand, cont.**
◆ <u>Define</u> Teachable Moments, using the information sheet. <u>Discuss</u> how teachable moments are times of shared interest and joy. Use the examples. ◆ Ask Parent to complete "Teachable Moments With My Baby." <u>Discuss</u> how routines create patterns for baby. Why do patterns provide confidence and safety? Why do babies learn from patterns? ◆ <u>Review</u> the information sheet "Routines Become Teachable Moments." ◆ Ask Parent to complete the "Family Routines" worksheet. ◆ <u>Present</u> "The Teaching Loop" as a skill that helps Parents initiate learning. Review the example and practice with baby, using a "Playing Is Learning" Activity Card you think will be effective.	<u>Patterns</u> Repetitions of a model; a continuous design; an expected procedure <u>Regulation</u> A rule or guide to help ensure success within a group. A way to help balance, keep operations in good order <u>Relationship</u> The emotional connection between two people <u>Scaffolding</u> Structuring for success; helping, supporting, and guiding, but...*not doing* the task <u>Teachable Moment</u> Anytime you and your baby interact, baby is learning something <u>Trust</u> Knowing another will be dependable, reliable, and safe to share your feelings (see <u>Love</u> Unit)

MATERIALS, SUPPLIES, & RESOURCES:

•<u>Love's Labors</u> video

•<u>The Developing Child</u>, H. E. Brisbane

•Pictures of faces, or construction paper and markers

•Ribbon; scissors; still pictures of babies, still pictures of parents.

•Video camera

INTERACTIVE SESSION

Activity: Parents practice a teachable moment during a caretaking routine using the teaching loop. The goal of this activity is for parents to practice each step of the loop and experience their child's response to each step.

Hints for Success

Parents will need to be familiar with steps in routines.

Practice the teaching loop.

Review ways to share interest and fun with baby.

Educator emphasizes success in the interaction, over the completion of the routine.

Set the Stage:

1. ◆Review the "Teaching Loop."

2. Make a poster of the teaching loop and place it on wall or bulletin board.

3. Choose an age-appropriate routine to practice during class or with a parent (e.g., putting on shoes and socks, diapering, feeding, snack time, etc.)

4. Review ways to make this fun for baby.

Supervised Interaction in Home Visits or in Parent Groups:

☆1. Practice a teachable moment during a caretaking routine using the teaching loop.
   2. See directions and procedures in Introduction (page vii).

Closure:

Review with each parent the videotaped session.
What did they think their baby learned? What did they think their baby enjoyed?
Parent completes: ◆"Activity Form" (see Appendix).

Expansion/Enrichment:

Encourage parents to apply the teaching loop when playing with baby in a teachable moment.

TOPIC:

Baby's First Teacher

For a Parent Group

1. Add topic poster, worksheets and information pages to parent's Play Portfolio.

2. Display or have articles available on trust, consistency, security.

3. Child care staff models the "Teaching Loop" during teachable moments.

4. ◆"Teaching Loop" poster displayed in nursery.

5. Create bulletin board which illustrates teachable moments with pictures. Have parents make comments on each example.

6. Parents demonstrate to another parent group or school class, using the ◆"Family Routines" worksheet, while focusing baby on fun and learning.

For Parents at Home

• Practice using the teaching loop at home.

• Observe other caregivers during a teachable moment. Analyze what the baby is learning.

• List steps to some caregiving routines. Post in nursery.

• Make a face mobile from black and white construction paper. Hang above baby's crib.

• Make a poster for the refrigerator or the baby's room telling how babies learn.
  Use patterned lettering like the ◆"Word Scramble" activity.

• Sometimes when babies are annoying their parents, parents can change this without anger by
  creating a teachable moment. Using ◆"DOOZYs" (Appendix), discuss with Home Visitor ways
  to do this.

People Prefer People When?

Answer the following questions by <u>circling the choice you prefer</u>.

1. When you call someone on the telephone, do you prefer a person or a tape to answer the phone?

2. When going to the grocery store, would you prefer a person to assist you in finding some item or a computer directory?

3. When sitting in a classroom would you prefer listening to a taped guest speaker or a real live person?

4. When changing your baby's diaper, do you think your baby would like you to act like a robot or a smiling faced person?

5. When watching a movie, do you prefer a human interest story or a story about making toothpicks?

6. Do you think your baby would rather listen to you singing a song or a taped lullaby?

Demonstrate or have parents try this:

Draw a picture of a face on a sheet of paper *or* find a picture of your face.
Place your picture and a rattle in front of your baby.
Perhaps hide behind the picture of the face.

Now ... which did your baby prefer, the picture of your face or the rattle? How could you tell?

Who Teaches Your Baby?

Who teaches your baby?

What might your infant learn from you?

Why are you the most important teacher for your baby?

How do you teach your baby?

When do you teach your baby?

WORD SCRAMBLE

Instructions for Word Scramble:
Pass out the scrambled letters on page 62 and explain:

1. Here are some letters on a page. What do these letters mean to you? Can you share this meaning with a friend?

2. Now rearrange these letters into something more understandable to all of us. Can you find a pattern for the letters that will have meaning for all of us?

   To do this, you will need to place the letters in a meaningful order—which we call "words." By ordering the letters into a pattern that is familiar for all of us, the meaning can be easily shared. Can you arrange these letters into four words?

After parents have worked on the task, explain:

3. The letters say "How do babies learn?"
   Each parent can color the letters or design their own word pattern for his or her baby's room.

Following this exercise, explain:

> ### All humans have a similar pattern to life.
> That is, most every home has a place to sleep, a place to "wash-up," a place to cook, to eat and to relax. Even when we are camping, we make these places. It is a basic pattern. Without a basic pattern, we feel disorganized and confused.
>
> ### Babies also need a basic pattern.
> Parents provide this through caretaking routines. By repeating the same procedure in the same way every day, shared meanings are learned. Our babies begin to share an understanding with us. They learn what to expect and this gives our babies a sense of safety and balance.
>
> ### Parents provide the 1st patterns in their babies' lives through routines.
> These become the first memories babies have. Routines are one of the first ways babies learn. Sharing routines helps establish trust and respect in a relationship.

Teachable Moments With My Baby

List below some activities you and your baby do often together (dressing, feeding, diapering, traveling, bed time). How could you make each one a fun and interesting experience for your baby?

List daily activities together	How can you make them teachable moments?
1.	
2.	
3.	
4.	
5.	

Teachable Moments

Babies are watching, listening, touching something with most every waking moment. This is one way they are learning about their world. They learn the most when they are sharing emotions with their parents. Dressing, eating, exercising, quiet times, and good night times are all times of emotional sharing. Every time you interact with your baby, the baby is learning something. Every moment with your baby is a teachable moment.

You are making a teachable moment

✿ **When you talk to a baby.**

✿ **When you share in the baby's interest.**

✿ **When you offer your baby something new to explore.**

✿ **When you find something exciting or surprising.**

As a parent, you can expand your baby's learning by sharing your feelings. Share something interesting . It is this feeling of fun that will focus your baby. Sharing positive feelings will organize your baby's nervous system for learning. Your baby will be more cooperative and more fun.

Example:

❖Get baby's attention with excitement.
Kevin, come with me. This will be fun!

❖Tell baby what you are going to do and share the task.
<u>*We*</u> *are going to fix lunch.*

❖Tell baby what is happening. What are your actions?
I'm going to put you up on the counter. Here we go!

❖Tell baby why with interest.
This way you can help me cook.

❖Show baby what you want.
Take this clean lettuce leaf. Tear it up, like this.
Now throw it into this bowl, like this.

❖Let baby try the task by himself.
Now you do it.

❖Use emotions and noises which are fun and exciting.
Yum, Yum, good for the Tum. YuMMMY

Family Routines Worksheet

Family routines are things that you and your baby expect to do every day or almost every day, like bathing, dressing, eating, snack time, making beds, getting in the car, feeding the dog, picking up toys, and bed time. What are some of your family routines?

- •Select a routine which you and your baby do often.
- •In the first column, make a list of the steps that are part of the routine.
- •In the next column, list how you might interact with your baby to make this routine fun, to make it new, to make it a teachable moment.
- •In the last column, list what baby might learn.

Family Routine for _____

A Family Routine... list steps in routine	**is a Teachable Moment.** list ways to share emotions	**Baby is always learning.** What is baby learning?

Routines Become Teachable Moments

A routine is something that happens over and over. It is usually something in our daily life that we do often. We begin to do it the same way every time. Or it is something that we are taught to do in order to share an understanding with another, such as addressing an envelope. It becomes a habit. For example: Putting your house keys on a hook by the door. This becomes a habit. You feel confident because you always know where your keys are. It is a feeling of safety.

Routines make us feel comfortable and safe, because we know what to expect. We know the procedure so well that we don't have to think about it. *We own it.* This means we can easily think about something else, like having fun with the baby!

An example: Diapering the Baby

Diapering Routine:	Making a Teachable Moment	Baby is learning...
1. Wash hands.	1. Tell baby what you're going to do.	1. Respect
2. Gently place baby on changing table.	2. Coo and talk to Baby as you put him on table.	2. Voice sounds
3. Place clean diaper under infant, before removing soiled diaper.	3. Divert Baby's attention with toy.	3. Interest
4. Remove soiled diaper. Put soiled diaper in plastic bag.	4. Play with Baby's toes.	4. Shared emotion
5. Use baby wipe to clean baby thoroughly.	5. Laugh and blow on tummy.	5. Surprise - sharing a new feeling
6. Fasten diaper securely.	6. Say, "There's your tummy" when you blow on it.	6. Body parts, words, laughter
7. Wash baby's hands.	7. "All done. You're clean."	7. Finale or ending word
8. Place baby in a secure, interesting area.	8. "I'll be right back."	8. Safety, patience, trust
9. Spray diapering area with disinfectant.	9. "You're OK; feeling clean and good."	9. Emotion regulation
10. Wash your hands. Then go to baby and pick baby up.	10. "OK! What's next?!"	10. Diapering isn't the only thing you share

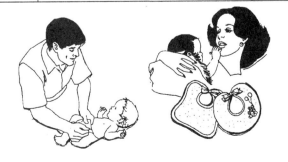

The Teaching Loop

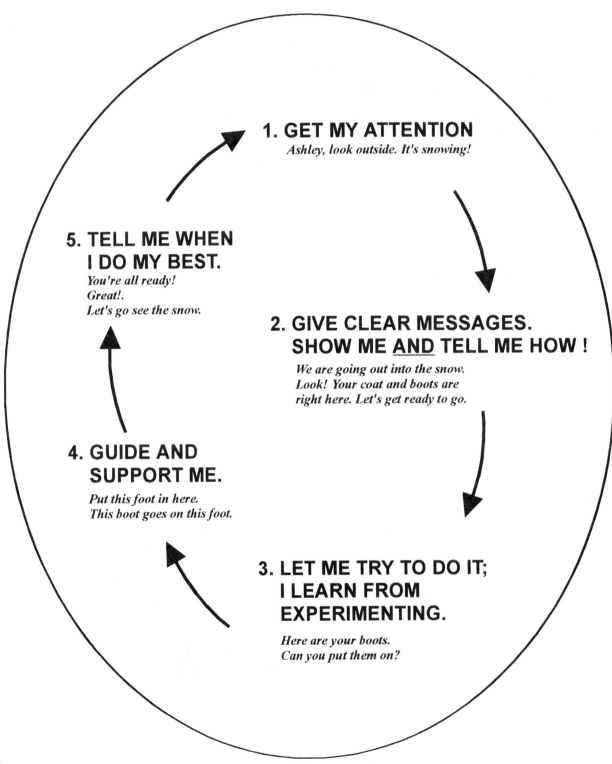

1. GET MY ATTENTION
Ashley, look outside. It's snowing!

2. GIVE CLEAR MESSAGES.
SHOW ME <u>AND</u> TELL ME HOW !
We are going out into the snow.
Look! Your coat and boots are
right here. Let's get ready to go.

3. LET ME TRY TO DO IT;
I LEARN FROM
EXPERIMENTING.
Here are your boots.
Can you put them on?

4. GUIDE AND
SUPPORT ME.
Put this foot in here.
This boot goes on this foot.

5. TELL ME WHEN
I DO MY BEST.
You're all ready!
Great!.
Let's go see the snow.

I Am ... Evaluation for Baby's First Teacher

Complete the following *I Am* statements.

1. *I am* my baby's first teacher because ...

2. *I am* using daily routines because ...

3. *I am* sharing positive emotions during routines because ...

4. *I am* helping my baby by sending clear messages because ...

5. *I am* letting baby try to do some things alone because ...

6. *I am* helping my baby communicate during daily routines by ...

7. *I am* building trust with my baby during daily routines by ...

TOPIC 4

What Are Babies Really Learning?

What Are Babies Really Learning?

1. <u>Relationships teach babies more than lessons</u>. Through their relationship with their parents, babies are really learning how to control their nervous systems and emotions, how to organize and focus their minds and how to behave so as to 'fit-in' and enjoy other humans. These are lessons of stabilization and socialization. These lessons will be different for every baby.

There is an incredible amount of learning that occurs in the first three years of life. Babies go from awkward sucking motions to peanut butter sandwiches, from coos and smiles to books and songs, from jerky movements to climbing and jumping. Much of this is biologically programmed. Parents do not teach their babies to reach, sit or crawl; these skills happen because of brain maturation. Developmental milestones are similar and predictable for most all babies. If babies are so similar, why are adults so different?

2. <u>Parents define uniqueness in their child</u>. Parents influence many of these differences. Parents provide the genetic make-up which determines differences in skin color, hair color, stature and temperament. These genes may also play a role in what babies will be good at, such as throwing a ball, writing a book, or being a musician. Parents define differences between babies by the nutrition they provide and by the routines they establish. Babies' schedules and surroundings influence their health and play a role in what they learn.

More importantly, parents provide the cocoon which surrounds, nurtures, and guides the baby's maturation and learning. In the first three years, the relationship with parents gives babies feelings of safety and protection, while also giving shape and structure to their lives. Parents regulate babies' temperament and emotion. They calm and comfort. They model and share positive feeling and actions. This relationship gives the stability which organizes babies' brains, maximizes development, and opens the doors to possibility.

3. <u>In the first year, parents provide the foundation for learning</u>. Parents ... who provide a safe nurturant place for babies to survive ... teach confidence and trust. Parents who share positive, calm emotions steady their babies' sensitive nervous systems. They teach self-control and balance. Parents who set patterns and schedules, give babies a sense of focus and structure. Parents who provide the human model for babies to copy, teach baby how to manage new people and new experiences. By guiding babies with appropriate toys and experiences, parents set small, reachable goals which give their babies feelings of mastery. Parents who provide praise and love, help their babies feel valued. This gives babies stability or balance.

4. <u>In the second and third year, parents teach and model social skills</u>. The lessons of the next two years are more complex. By the end of the first year, most babies are trying to walk and beginning to say words. There is a strong spurt in initiative. "What can I do? How far can I go? What are all of these things in my world?" The toddler is experimenting with power. "How do I affect others? How do I get what I want? " "What if I say NO?"

Many of the lessons learned during these years are about social skills. Parents are teaching their toddlers how to "fit in" and belong with other humans. When parents regulate their toddler's emotional swings, they are teaching self-control. Parents who sometimes allow their toddlers to feel independent and powerful are teaching competence and problem solving. And when parents know *how* and *when* to limit toddlers, they are teaching respect.

As toddlers begin learning words, parents are teaching meanings. They teach their toddlers how to clearly express their needs and to negotiate their wants. Parents teach their toddlers how to use others as helpers. They teach their toddlers how to cooperate and to share. Parents show toddlers how to be patient and how to understand about others' feelings. Their toddlers are learning about empathy and conscience. In the first three years, parents define their child's basic sense of values: the do's and don'ts of living together. This is called socialization.

5. <u>How parents teach defines how babies will learn</u>. The differences in how parents teach and model behavior will make a lasting difference in how their babies continue to learn. Teaching styles can give confidence and make learning exciting or they can confuse and inhibit learning. Differences in motivation to learn, in ability to focus and in persistence are initiated within the relationships of the first three years.

Often parents have learned their teaching styles from their own parents. Some have copied grandparents, some have watched teachers and mentors they like. Today we know much more about how babies learn in these early years. We can offer parents new information and different styles to use. The mentoring styles (scaffolding, supporting and instructing) are the best ways to encourage learning. Changing a parent's teaching style is not easy. It takes commitment and practice.

•How do early relationships influence learning?
•What are babies learning during this time?
•Do differences in the way parents teach affect this learning?
•Why is socialization important to learn from parents?

What Are Babies Really Learning?

Outcomes:

1. Parents will be able to describe what babies are learning from the parent-infant relationship during the first three years.
2. Parents will demonstrate a teaching style which fosters learning.

Content and Concepts	Instructional Strategies for Parent Groups
INTRODUCTION:	Display Instructor's Building Block #4 (see pg. 71)
❖ We learn through relationships. • When we share with another person, we learn about their feelings. -Likes and dislikes -Motivations and goals. -Opinions and habits -Attitudes and values	During a relationship we learn from one another. Using clay/play dough, ask parents to work the clay to get "acquainted" with it. How will their relationship with the clay affect what they make? Now ask parents to model an object. Discuss how different each object is. Could they learn anything about each other from seeing these?
KEY CONCEPTS: ❖ The first relationship is the foundation for learning. • Babies learn the most from their Relationships with their parents. • Parents provide protection, nurturance, structure, and the model for learning. • Parents provide the emotional connection which maximizes learning.	Ask parent to imagine an over-stuffed chair. "How do you feel in this chair?" (*relaxed, invited, supported*) Now imagine a hard, straight-backed chair. "How do you feel in this chair?" (*alert, focused, on-edge*). These chairs are metaphors for how different relationships support different feelings. Using clay, model your favorite chair. How do you feel in this chair? Protected, relaxed? Can you feel social, interested? Can you read or learn here? Can you express anger or jump for joy? How are parents like this chair?
❖ In the first year, babies learn stability. • Confidence: "I will survive." • Trust: "I am protected." • Belonging: "I have a model and guide." • Balance: "I have help, I am 'in tune.'" • Structure: "I remember, I'm learning." • Love: "I'm Valued."	◆ Use transparency and Information sheet: "Stability" and "Relationships Give Stability," discuss each block and how these feelings provide the right situation for learning.

Instructional Strategies for Home Visitors	**Terms to Understand**
We learn through relationships. <u>Take turns with parent, sharing your dreams</u> for a vacation. How are your ideas and dreams the same? different? Did you learn about one another from sharing in this way?	<u>Appropriate</u> Especially suitable or fitting for baby's developmental or emotional level <u>Assurance</u> Guarantee; feeling sure and safe; being confident of parents' protection and guidance
<u>Ask parent</u> to imagine an over-stuffed chair. "How do you feel in this chair?" (*relaxed, invited, supported*) <u>Now imagine</u> a hard, straight-backed chair. "How do you feel in this chair?" (*alert, uncomfortable, on-edge*). These chairs are metaphors for how relationships convey meaning because of shared feelings. <u>Using clay or play dough</u>, each of you mold your favorite chair. Discuss what this chair might mean, why might this chair become a favorite? How is the chair like a parent?	<u>Commitment</u> A pledge to do something; a promise to be there as baby's base of safety <u>Emotional Connectedness</u> Linked emotionally; sharing the same feelings <u>Nurturant</u> One who nourishes or feeds; giving baby emotional attention and affection
◆<u>Discuss</u> key concepts in "Relationships Give Stability." Explore with parents the experiences they provide which help create stability and allow Learning to happen. Use handout ◆"Stability" to illustrate.	<u>Organized nervous system</u> Having nerves calm and nerve connections functioning effectively

Content and Concepts	Instructional Strategies for Parent Groups
❖In the second year, babies learn socialization. 　•Behavior regulation: "I know the rules." 　•Emotional control: "My parents will help me." 　•Negotiation: "I can use words." 　•Social Skills: "I can take turns, share, join." 　•Independence: "I can explore more, 　　master more. 　•Balance: "I'm OK, I'm valued, I can make it."	◆<u>Use Transparency and information sheet</u>, "Socialization" and "The Second and Third Year." Define socialization as "fitting in" or belonging to a group. How are socialization and survival connected? How does socialization advance learning? <u>Discuss each block</u>. How do parents help babies learn these skills? Why do these blocks lead to balance and resiliency?
❖Teaching styles can help or hinder learning. 　•Parents guide and model learning. 　•They teach through shared emotions. 　•They give meaning to developmental change. 　•They use patterns and set limits.	<u>Have parent recall his or her worst and best teacher.</u> <u>Make a list</u> of "why" for each teacher. ◆Using Information Sheet "Teaching Styles," discuss: 　- how this teacher might be categorized 　- what was learned from this teacher on the relationship 　　level? ("I'm a smart person." "I'm a poor student.") 　- how did they feel in this teacher's classroom? ◆<u>Analyze</u> "Teaching Styles." Then <u>role play</u> "Which Style Is This?" and answer the set questions for each statement.
❖Parents can use many teaching styles. 　•They will use many styles during a day. 　•They can also mix styles. 　•Practicing new styles gives parents more 　　choice in teaching and regulating baby's 　　behavior. 　•The mentoring styles, through practice, 　　become habits.	◆With "Teaching Styles," analyze the components 　of the mentoring styles. Why do these lead to learning? ◆Ask parents to learn the "Scaffolding Style." ◆Use "Scaffolding Techniques" to teach this and discuss age-appropriate differences in Peg Board Activity.

Demonstration:

Demonstrate the scaffolding technique, using a baby between 9 and 20 months of age and a Peg Board game.

Discuss, as you are playing with the baby, how you are scaffolding for success.

(See ◆"Scaffolding Techniques.")

Evaluation/Closure

Complete ◆"Checking What I Have Learned."

Instructional Strategies for Home Visitors	**Terms to Understand, cont.**
<u>Discuss</u> how socialization is accomplished through the parent-child relationship. Ask parent to reflect on ways in which his or her parent (or surrogate) provided a model for making friends. Were these good experiences? What kind of model do they want to provide their child? Use teaching aids ♦ "Socialization" and "The Second and Third Year."	<u>Perfectionistic</u> Wanting baby to be without fault; expecting too much too soon <u>Resiliency</u> Ability to find balance, regain equilibrium, recover or adjust easily
<u>Have parent recall his or her worst and best teacher.</u> <u>Make a list</u> of "why" for each teacher. ♦Using Information Sheet "Teaching Styles," discuss: - how this teacher might be categorized - what was learned from this teacher on the relationship level? ("I'm a smart person," "I'm a poor student.") - how did they feel in this teacher's classroom? ♦<u>Explore worksheet</u>: "Which Style Is This?" <u>Discuss</u>: How parents may use all styles with a baby. Which styles lead to learning for baby? (particularly analyze mentoring styles). ♦Present the "Scaffolding Technique." Apply it with parent in an age-appropriate activity.	<u>Socialization</u> Learning to fit into a group; understanding their rules and patterns. Being able to share emotions and ideas with others <u>Stability</u> A feeling of balance; parents help baby learn balance <u>Structure</u> Arrange in a definite pattern or organization; provide pathways and guidelines for baby <u>Uniqueness</u> Being the only one; very special or unusual

MATERIALS, SUPPLIES, & RESOURCES:

•Clay or play dough for each parent

•Peg Board game—can make one or use commercial toy

•Video Camera

•Additional activity card suggestions from <u>Listen</u> and <u>Love</u> PIPE units

INTERACTIVE SESSION

Activity: Parents practice scaffolding technique with their babies, using several age-appropriate activities. The goal for this activity is for parents to experience a sense of teaching by supporting baby's exploration and interest areas.

Hints for Success

Parents will need to be familiar with steps in the technique.

Parents will need to plan ahead for success in the activity. Baby's state. appropriate toys, etc.

If baby is not interested in your toy, introduce a choice of other activities. Let baby choose.

Try scaffolding with baby's choice of activity.

Set the Stage:

1. Review the scaffolding technique.

2. Make a poster of the mentoring teaching styles and post it on the wall.

3. Discuss how the scaffolding technique can be used in Teachable Moments as well as in a play activity.

4. Discuss how the emotions you share will give baby stability to focus and learn.

Supervised Interaction in Home Visits or in Parent Groups:

☆1. Practice the scaffolding technique, letting baby lead. Focus baby with your emotions.
2. See directions and procedures in the Introduction (page vii).

Closure:

Review with each parent the video taped session. Or discuss what he or she thought baby had learned. Was the technique easy to do with baby? What did baby enjoy?

Expansion/Enrichment:

Encourage parents to try the scaffolding technique at home. Combine it with the teaching loop. Bring stories to class about how you have applied the loop with other teaching styles.

TOPIC:

What Are Babies Really Learning?

For a Parent Group

1. Add topic poster, worksheets and information pages to parent's Play Portfolio.

2. Make posters for the child care center for ◆"Stabilization" and ◆"Socialization."

3. Make a mobile of Stabilization Blocks to hang at home.

4. Have a "meet 'n' greet" party where you ask grandparents or another child care group to come join in group play. Model for your baby how to meet strangers and share toys. Stay focused on the babies, not on parent-to-parent conversations.

5. In a "Reporter's Notebook," for two days take notes about the "Teaching Styles" you observe in class, child care center, in shopping center and at home. Discuss these notes with your class-mates. Which style did you observe the most?

For Parents at Home

• Make posters for your room about stabilization. Place the poster where it will be a reminder. Congratulate yourself by putting a star on the poster when you do one of these things with your baby.

• Discuss with home visitor and other family members how babies learn to get along in a family. What are some family rules and limits?

• When you and your baby are out, practice sharing something positive with others, even strangers. Observe how baby watches you.

• Plan a family party (e.g. cookies and apple juice before bed). Have everyone show cele-bration by modeling sharing, courtesy, helping, waiting to eat, etc.

• When babies feel unsure or are learning the rules of a group, they may do things which annoy their parents. Using ◆"DOOZYs" (see Appendix), discuss with your home visitor some examples and solutions.

The First Year:
Relationships Give Stability

The first year is a time of survival and rapid change. Babies are learning about how their bodies work. Every day a new nerve connection is made and a new ability is gained. Imagine how confusing it would be if everything you knew and did was different every day.

Babies need a sense of stability in their changing world.
Who will help them find equilibrium or balance?

❖ Parents provide the stable base which surrounds and nurtures babies through the first year.

❖ Parents are the emotional connection which will organize or disorganize baby's learning.

❖ Parents are the guide, setting patterns and expectations for learning.

Parents provide protection, warmth and nutrition, which allow development and learning

For example: A newborn needs to know when to expect food and sleep. Parents set a schedule which allows babies' bodies to become regulated. This gives babies physical stability. Now, learning can begin.

Parents regulate emotional extremes which strengthens pathways for learning.

For example: A newborn who sleeps close to mother develops her breathing rhythms and her sleeping patterns. When parents hold their babies close, their babies calm to their body rhythms. This helps to stabilize a baby's exploding nervous system. Babies also share the emotional rhythms of their parents. A positive emotional "shared space" organizes and connects babies to learning. As they were in the womb, babies remain "one" with their first relationships.

Parents allow and support the mastery cycle.

For example: A newborn begins to smile voluntarily between one and two months. When parents return the smile, a connection is made. Babies practice smiling and learn how others respond. A playful pattern is established. The baby is feeling mastery. The baby feels valued.

Parents guide and structure babies' learning.

For example: As babies begin to develop, parents plan ahead, set the stage and define the structure for babies. "We always take a bath before dinner." "We always play the music box before bed." Parents set routines which become expected procedures in babies' memories. These give babies a sense of constancy and continuity. Some of this "procedural knowledge" stays with babies for a lifetime.

----··· Stability ----··

- ❖ **The first relationship is the Foundation for Learning.**

- ❖ **Parents provide the feelings of stability which allow learning to occur.**

These feelings are:

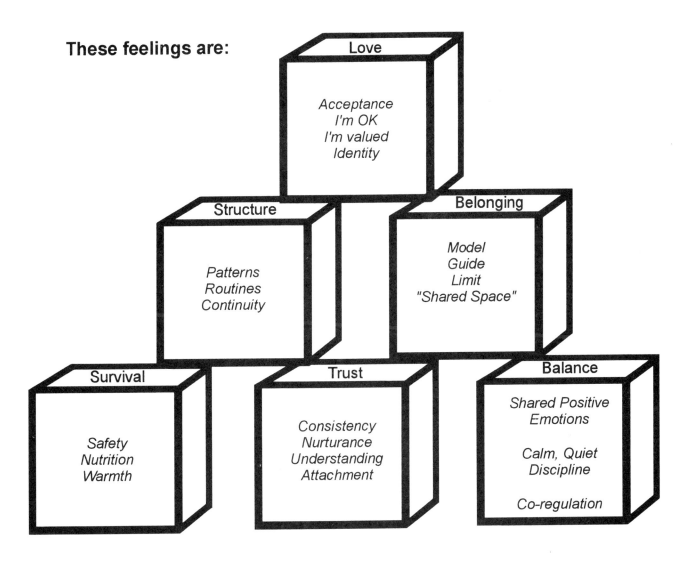

The Second/Third Year:
Relationships Teach Socialization

The second year is the age of Initiative. Babies become toddlers. They start to walk and talk. They are more assertive and willful. "How do I get what I want?" "Can I influence the people around me?" They are experimenting with relationships. "What if I don't do what I'm told?" "How do I manage my fear and my anger?" "Where do I 'fit in' with other people?" "Am I valued; am I loved?"

By the third year, Toddlers begin to master skills; they have learned rules and limits; they know who smiles and who growls. Using a memory image of their parents (like a teddy bear), they can be independent. They will take their patterns forward to new relationships and learning.

Who will show them how to behave, how to have empathy, how to value others?

✤ Parents are the first model of how to live with and enjoy other people.
✤ Parents demonstrate how to manage emotions and deal with frustrations.
✤ Parents celebrate the positives, giving babies resiliency.

Parents show babies how to meet and enjoy other people.

For example: Babies copy their parents' faces, voice tones, and actions. They watch their parents intently to learn how to behave. When parents are friendly with others, babies learn to make friends. When parents use words more than actions, babies learn to negotiate and collaborate. Babies join into a "shared space" with parents to learn how to relate to others.

Parents demonstrate how to manage emotions.

For example: The second and third year are times of exploration for toddlers with little information in memory. Toddlers are "in trouble" or danger every few minutes. They become very angry or frightened quickly and cannot regain balance. Parents steady babies' emotions and teach them calm, clear alternatives.

Parents teach the do's and don'ts of behavior.

For example: Toddlers really want to please their parents. Toddlers copy actions more than they listen to or understand words. When parents "join-in" with toddlers, they can show them what they want. By setting positive examples, "This is what we do," parents help baby master the rules and learn to "fit in" with others.

Parents model life skills.

For example: They show babies how to eat, brush teeth, bathe and dress. They show toddlers how to focus their attention, how to read and write, how to use the phone. What interests a parent will shape what toddler will like. These are "shared spaces."

— ·—·· Socialization —·—··

❖ **The first relationship sets the pattern for all others.**

❖ **By modeling and teaching, parents show baby how to belong and learn from others.**

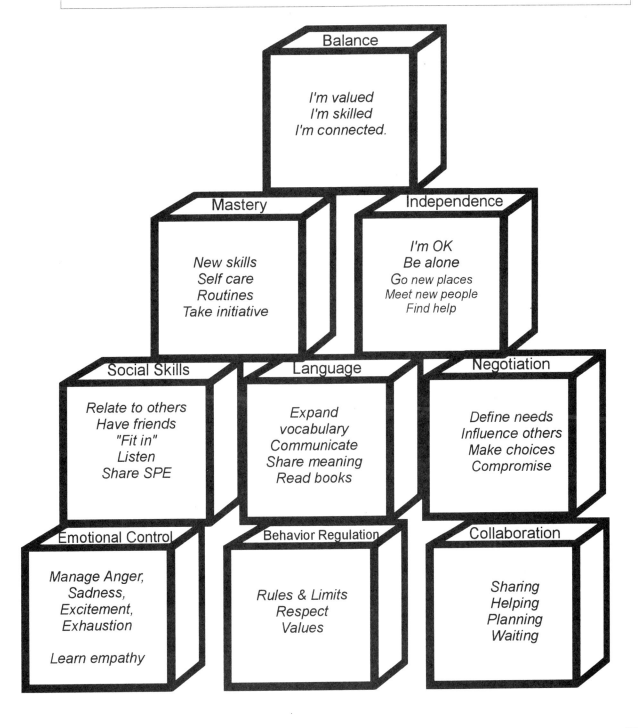

Balance

I'm valued
I'm skilled
I'm connected.

Mastery

New skills
Self care
Routines
Take initiative

Independence

I'm OK
Be alone
Go new places
Meet new people
Find help

Social Skills

Relate to others
Have friends
"Fit in"
Listen
Share SPE

Language

Expand
vocabulary
Communicate
Share meaning
Read books

Negotiation

Define needs
Influence others
Make choices
Compromise

Emotional Control

Manage Anger,
Sadness,
Excitement,
Exhaustion

Learn empathy

Behavior Regulation

Rules & Limits
Respect
Values

Collaboration

Sharing
Helping
Planning
Waiting

Which Style Is This?

The way we teach has lots to do with how babies learn.

Role play each example dialogue. Then for each example, answer the series of questions below.
1) What is the message? 2) What did baby learn? 3) What emotion might be in the parent's voice?
4) What might baby be feeling?   5) What do you think baby might do?
6) Discuss which teaching style this might be. Why?

"I want it clean here. Pick up the blocks... Quickly! One...Two...Three."
"Sweetheart, Gramma is coming. .... Should we pick up?"
"These need to be picked up .... but I'll do it later."
"Pick up these blocks or you're gonna get it!"
"We can go out as soon as the blocks are picked up. .... Let's make it a game, I'll go first; now it's your turn. Wheee!!"
"Let's pick up the blocks. .... They go just this way. Put the red block in this spot."

Playing Is Learning

Teaching Styles

Learning Lots	Learning Little	Learning Lost
MENTORING	**CONFUSING**	**HURTFUL**
Babies feel interest/mastery.	Babies feel confused or bored.	Babies feel afraid, angry, defeated.

*Scaffolding Style**

Invest baby in a task
Support baby's ideas
Simplify tasks
Suggest next step
Keep baby focused
Guide toward mastery
Praise baby's successes

Mixed Message Style

Use questions, not
statements
No single focus
Give too many messages
Sound unconvincing
Don't follow through
Don't look at baby
Suggest too many tasks

Threatening Style

Threaten child
Anger quickly
Don't share tasks
Expectations too high
No PDP awareness
Don't follow through
Blame baby

Supportive Style

Plan ahead, prepare area,
let baby choose task
Join baby's interest area
Take turns with baby -
Expand task
Let baby try to get it
Let baby feel pride

Forgiving Style

Ask baby to do a task
Then do it for baby
Divert baby to new toys
Don't set limits
Don't focus - don't share
Don't follow through

Controlling Style

Demand—
"Do it my way"
"Use this toy"
Talk about own needs
Choose the task - ignore
baby's choice
Be impatient, blame baby

Instructive Style

Find interesting tasks or
have baby help in adult
tasks
Make tasks a game
Teach about the task
Use interest to focus baby
Give baby autonomy with
tasks

Nagging/Blaming Style

Give orders - point out
mistakes
Don't model/demonstrate
Don't follow through
Give verbal barrage
Don't take action or set limits
Leave job undone

Perfectionist Style

Your needs come first
Expect too much
Demand your way
Don't experiment
Don't explore
Don't show playfulness
Be impatient
Baby is rarely good enough

*See Scaffolding information sheets

Scaffolding Technique

What Is A Scaffold?

A scaffold is a super structure around another structure to give it temporary stability.
A scaffold gives support during developmental changes.
A scaffold allows changes to be made easily and safely.

Parents are like a scaffold.

They gently support the child to try something new.
They do not take over, but add stability to child's efforts.
They offer praise each step, giving confidence to the child.
They give support or comfort when child is unsure.

Techniques for scaffolding:

- Structure for success (safe place, good timing, right toys)
- Divide problems into "do-able" tasks.
- Start baby with easy, familiar task.
- Demonstrate (model) a new skill
- Give little rewards, often ("that's good)
- Give baby the next best step for success
- Allow baby to try and experiment
- Never scold. .... Ignore mistakes.
- Fix problems without pointing them out.
- Extend the task.
- If baby "tunes out," *quit.*
- Do not finish the task for baby. Leave it undone.
- Reward baby for the effort. ("You did a good job.")

Scaffolding is used by Coaches, Mentors, and Support persons.
It fosters learning.

Scaffolding Technique with Peg Board

A scaffolding example using the Peg Board Task (see Topic 2)

9 month old

Baby picks up a dowel. Parent lets baby finger the peg and chew on it. Parent holds out her hand to baby as if to ask for a dowel. If baby gives it to parent, she hands it back. This becomes a turn-taking game which brings laughter and fun. Parent can extend this game by putting a dowel in each of the baby's hands.

Parent starts rolling the dowel on the floor. Baby smiles and looks at parent who smiles back. Parent waits to let baby explore this play on his or her own, if baby is having fun.

Parent then turns the box top over and puts some dowels inside. Parent dumps them out and hands one to the baby and says, "Here, you do it." If baby does it, parent praises baby. If baby doesn't seem interested, parent says nothing. Picks up dowels and joins in baby's interest.

12 month old

Mom shows baby how to put a peg in the hole in the box top. Baby takes peg out. Mom laughs. "Now put it in." Mom waits while Baby struggles, then Mom guides the bottom of the peg into the hole and says,"There! You did it!" She hands baby another peg and helps guide it into the hole. Then she sits back and watches baby experiment with other holes for the same peg. When baby tires, Mom says, "Let's put this away." She picks up pegs, puts them in the box and sets them up before getting a new toy for the baby. Baby watches.

15 month old

Dad gives baby all the pegs and puts the box top in front. He says, "Look what I have. Put the pegs in here like this." He puts in a peg. Baby takes peg out and puts another one in. Dad smiles and says "Great!" Baby takes peg out and puts another one in the same hole. Dad hands baby another peg and says, "Put this one in here." He helps guide the next peg to a new hole. Then dad sits back and smiles while baby puts the rest of the pegs in their holes. Baby smiles and claps. Then dad says, "Good deal. Give me a high-five!" Dad takes out the pegs and says, " Do you want to go again?" Baby tries about half the pegs and then walks away. Dad puts pegs away.

Date: _____

Name _____

Topic _____

<u>Checking What I Learned</u>

1. Define what babies learn the first year?

2. Define what babies learn the second year?

3. Explain and name the examples of the <u>mentoring</u> teaching styles.

4. Which style(s) is/are most suited for you and your baby?

TOPIC 5

Learning
the "Do's"

Learning the "Do's"

1. <u>Socialization is learned through Play</u>. Play is a way we can feel a sense of connection with other humans. There are shared goals which require cooperation and communication. Play is a way new members can be integrated into a group. It is also a way to learn the rules and expectations of others. Play provides a feeling of belonging, a positive sense of "team."

2. <u>The family is like a team</u>. Parents establish the shared goals and family rules for babies. In the first year, a sense of belonging and structure comes through the nurturance, guidance and modeling which is part of the parent-infant relationship. But in the second year, when infants become toddlers, they also become independent, willful, and curious. They seem to want to test the family rules but also want to master the rules of belonging to the "family team." Parents now need to teach the "do's and don'ts" of family behavior and of the broader social world.

3. <u>Learning the "Do's" is like learning the rules of a game</u>. Babies want desperately to belong to and to please the members of the "family team." They enjoy showing off their knowledge of how to "fit-in" and behave. By knowing what "to do," babies often avoid the pitfalls of what "not to do." They avoid being scolded or embarrassed. Teaching a toddler that "we <u>do</u> hang up our coat" and providing an easy place to <u>do</u> this will eliminate the coat being dropped on the floor and the toddler being corrected. Parents who teach the "do's" will have children who feel that they can master the rules of the household. They have learned what "to do" to please their parents and to belong to "the family team."

4. <u>Learning patterns is part of learning the "do's."</u> Doing the same thing in the same way every time sets a pattern which babies learn to expect. They will plan to do what is expected, such as "we wash our hands before eating," "we sit in our chairs to eat," "wait until I cut your food." Babies will test the pattern several times and then expect to follow it. Most babies get upset and disorganized when their expected routine is not followed.

5. <u>"We" is a magic word for babies</u>. Babies view themselves as "one" with their parents; therefore, using the word "we" is more convincing than the word "you." "We are going to bed," "we do brush our teeth," "we sleep tight, full of love." Parents who join in with their baby or ask their baby to join with them are strengthening a sense of family team.

6. <u>Positive emotion empowers all of us</u>. We hardly know we are learning when we are having fun. When we share fun, interest, surprise or contentment with other people, we feel close and we feel valued. We are eager to collaborate, try new things, accept challenges. We become helpful and cooperative. This is why it is important to practice using positive language and positive emotions with babies whenever possible. Finding the bright side, laughing about mistakes, and problem solving with fun become habits that are contagious. The whole family may be more positive and playful.

Children raised with more positive emotion are better behaved and more psychologically stable. They are less apt to be violent, more successful in school, with their friends and other adults. Positive emotional connectedness is what makes us feel OK. We feel valued, even if we make mistakes. This gives us internal stability: "I know I am worthy of being loved." "I know I can learn to do things well to please myself and my parents."

7. <u>Toddlers are anxious to keep this positive feeling of connectedness.</u> They struggle to "get it right." They want approval. When parents take the time to thank toddlers for knowing the rules, they are sharing the joy together. Praise is a powerful way to teach a child. Parents' approval is remembered more often than parents' scoldings.

8. <u>Toddlers need special understanding.</u> Patterns that have been set in the first year may be lost in the second. Ten-month-old Sarah will point to a light plug and shake her head "no," but at 12 months of age, she will crawl over and touch it, then look at her parent and laugh. The toddler's strong drive for exploration and mastery has expanded to one of experimentation. "What will happen if ...?"

9. <u>Turn negatives into positives.</u> Often naughty behaviors in a toddler can be ignored, diverted, or re-directed without using negative emotions or "don'ts." Behaviors that parents ignore, go away. Behaviors that parents divert are often forgotten. Behaviors that parents join, become positive. When the family becomes a "team" with a winning goal in mind, negative behaviors can be easily re-directed into positive actions. This is how child rearing becomes an interesting, playful challenge.

•Why do we learn more when we are having fun?
•How do shared positive emotions (SPE) empower us?
•Do happy families raise more successful children?
•How do we guide babies toward good behavior?
•How do we regulate behavior we don't like?

Learning the "Do's"

Outcomes:

1. Parents can analyze how play helps baby develop cooperation and collaboration skills.
2. Parents will plan a pattern for an activity which will help baby learn the "do's."
3. Parents will use the power of shared positive emotions to teach the "do's."
4. Parents will recognize benefits of teaching the "do's" to manage a toddler's willfulness.

Content and Concepts	Instructional Strategies for Parent Groups
INTRODUCTION:	Display Instructor's Building Block #5 (see pg. 89)
❖ Play is one way to learn socialization.	Have parents play a team game
• When we share fun	(e.g. Pictionary or ◆Triangle Task)
-we collaborate easily	Discuss:
-we become a team	• how goals were shared
-we learn rules	• how rules were accepted easily
-we share goals	(e.g., take turns, share ideas, majority rules)
	How is being on a team like a family or community?
• Play teaches the rules or "do's and don'ts" of belonging to a team or a family.	Watch babies at play or review the PIPE video. Discuss rules (the "Do's and Don'ts") baby is learning through play.
KEY CONCEPTS:	
❖ Patterns teach the "do's" to baby.	Review the concept of a pattern (a habit, a routine, a set of rules) as something that has a shared meaning and makes a goal easier.
• Patterns help babies master the shared goals and rules of a family team.	◆ Worksheet "A Pattern I Use."
• Babies become disorganized, fuss, or misbehave without structure or pattern.	Identify a patterned activity for a baby or toddler.
	◆ Handout: "The Do's: Helping Baby Learn a Pattern."
• The most effective learning occurs when parents join Baby and work or play as a team.	Discuss how parent and baby need to share this pattern and work as a team.
	◆ Worksheet: "Building a Pattern Together."

Instructional Strategies for Home Visitors	Terms to Understand
<u>Play a simple game with the parent</u>, such as Hangman or a simple card game. <u>Discuss:</u> • how rules were accepted easily • how goals were shared How is playing together on a team like a family or community?	Collaborate To work easily with another; willingly assist or share Consistent Showing steady sameness; always repeating the same pattern
Review the PIPE video. Discuss rules (the "Do's and Don'ts") baby is learning through play. ◆ Use Worksheet: "Baby's Favorite Play" to give insight into how babies fit into a group by learning the "do's and don'ts" through play.	Contagious Spreading rapidly, as emotional expressions quickly influence others Disorganized nervous system Anxious, nervous, unable to gain calm or focus. Babies are fussy, whiny, have tantrums, suck thumbs, run around wildly.
<u>Review the concept</u> of a pattern (a habit, a routine, a set of rules) as something that has a shared meaning and makes a goal easier. <u>Ask parents to describe</u> a pattern which they use often (getting dressed, putting on make up, etc.). -Ask parent what the benefits of a pattern are. ◆See "A Pattern I Use."	Distracted Turned aside, confused, drawn away from a task
◆Handout: "The Do's: Helping Baby Learn a Pattern." Discuss an example of how parent and baby need to share patterns. ◆Worksheet: "Building a Pattern Together."	Divert To turn away, change someone's attention or focus

Content and Concepts	Instructional Strategies for Parent Groups

❖ Emotional signals drive most learning.
  • Shared Positive Emotions (SPE) are powerful tools for teaching collaboration and cooperation.
  • SPE makes learning the "do's" easy.
  • Babies raised with more SPE are better behaved.
	Explain: How SPE enhances learning and affects family patterns.
	◆ Use Info. Sheet: "The Power of Positive Emotions."
	◆ Show transparency: "Positive Emotions Propel Learning" Practice expressing positive emotions.
	◆ Discuss worksheet: "Fun Can Regulate Behavior."

❖ Teaching the "do's" allows the "don'ts" to be used sparingly.
  • "We" is a magic word for babies.
	◆ Discuss: "A+ Ideas for Teaching the Do's" Stress the importance of being a team and using "We Do's."
	◆ Role play: "Turning Don'ts Into We Do's."
	  • Use "We-do's" - "We do buckle our seat belt."
	    • Model - "See Daddy do it."
	    • Use clear, calm discipline - "No, no. Sit down. "
	    • Divert - "Look! See the bird. Zoom. Zoom."
	  Be sure expectations fit baby's ability.

❖ Toddlers need understanding.
 	
  • Toddlerhood is a time of initiative and experimentation.
  • Challenging parents is a mastery task.
  • Testing rules is a learning game.
  • Ignoring, diverting, re-directing are good tools for teaching the "do's."
	◆ Have parents read and fill in blanks: "How Do You Describe a Toddler?" (see Key below) Discuss the initiative and experimentation of toddlerhood.
	
	Show Magna System Video: Toddlerhood, Emotional Development.
	
	◆ Handout: "Turning 'Don'ts' Into 'We-do's.'"

Demonstration:

Demonstrate how to get baby to do something or change focus by using Shared Positive Emotions (SPE). Use some A+ Ideas to regulate baby's behavior.

Evaluation/Closure

  ◆ "How Babies Learn the 'Do's'"

Key to "How Do You Describe a Toddler?"

1. explorer	6. five
2. exhausting	7. "twos"
3. challenge	8. model
4. power	9. safe
5. excitement	10. ignore

Instructional Strategies for Home Visitors	Terms to Understand, cont.
<u>Explain</u>: How SPE enhances learning and influences family patterns. Use ◆"The Power of Positive Emotions" and ◆"Positive Emotions Propel Learning."	<u>The "DO's"</u> Something we always do; a set pattern or rule; an expected event
◆<u>Complete and discuss worksheet</u>: "Fun Regulates Behavior."	<u>Frustrated</u> Discouraged, defeated, insecure; angry

◆<u>Discuss</u>: "A+ Ideas for Teaching the Do's"
 	
<u>Role play examples of Teaching the Do's</u>.
   •Use "We-do's" - "We <u>do</u> buckle our seat belt."
   •Model - "See Daddy do it."
   •Use clear, calm discipline - "No, no. Sit down."
   •Divert - "Look! See the bird. Zoom. Zoom."
Be sure expectations fit baby's ability.
	<u>Habit</u>
	Something we do regularly without thinking about it
	
	<u>Oppositional</u>
	Testing the rules, denying requests, doing the opposite of what is wanted

◆<u>Read outloud and discuss</u>: "How Do You Describe a Toddler?" Fill in the missing words. <u>Discuss</u> the initiative and experimentation of toddlerhood. ◆ <u>Assist parent with worksheet</u>: "Turning Don'ts Into 'We-do's.'" Ask parent to select one to practice before the next visit.	<u>Re-direct</u> Change focus or direction; give baby a new idea or pathway <u>SPE</u> Sharing Positive Emotions

MATERIALS, SUPPLIES, & RESOURCES:

•Game or activity for introductory activity

•Items for demonstrating "the do's"

•VCR

•Magna Systems video <u>Toddlerhood, Emotional Development</u>

INTERACTIVE SESSION

Activity: Practice an activity in which "learning the do's" and Shared Positive Emotions are used. The goal of this activity is for the parent and baby to share ownership in a routine and for parents to use SPE to engage baby as a partner in a pattern of events.

Hints for Success

Monitor and encourage use of "do's" and SPE, sharing joy, fun, surprise and interest.

With toddlers 12-36 months help parents see how babies can help with the routine.

Videotape session.

Set the Stage:

1. ◆Review handouts "The Do's: Helping Baby Learn A Pattern" and "A+ Ideas for Teaching the Do's."

2. Assist parent in choosing an age-appropriate activity which involves learning a routine.

3. Using handout ◆"The Do's: Helping Baby Learn a Pattern," involve baby in the implementation of the interactive session routine. Babies can watch; toddler can help get out and put away.

4. <u>For Home Visitors:</u>
   Review and discuss the routine currently used for the interactive session. In collaboration with the parent examine the procedure for future interactive sessions to make it fit parent's and family needs.

Supervised Interaction in Home Visits or Parent Groups:

☆ 1. Practice using SPE to teach a routine to baby. Find ways to let baby help with the routine (getting out, putting away, etc.)
2. See directions and procedures in the Introduction (page vii).

Closure:

Review Video tape with parent.
◆Review handout: "Fun (SPE) Leads to Learning." Discuss how baby responded to the use of SPE. What worked? What didn't?

Expansion/Enrichment:

Continue to practice SPE to teach the "do's." Develop a set pattern for you and baby to follow during other daily activities.

TOPIC ENHANCERS

TOPIC:

Learning the "Do's"

For a Parent Group

1. Add topic poster, worksheets and information pages to parent's Play Portfolio.
2. Display toys, games, and activities which can help baby learn the "do's."
3. Child care provider models/explains techniques used in a child care setting to teach the "do's."
4. Discuss with child care provider ages when babies can begin to learn a pattern. List some small, early patterns.
5. Display magazine articles, pamphlets, etc. which offer guidelines for using Shared Positive Emotions (SPE) to direct behavior. Discuss with parents.
6. Create bulletin board "Building Blocks for Teaching the Do's" or "Fun (SPE) Leads to Learning." Highlight techniques from the handouts or lesson worksheets.
7. Try Shared Positive Emotions with other family members or friends. What were the results? Report back to class.

For Parents at Home

- Make signs on 3" x 5" cards or make magnets to use on refrigerator, in the car, or other areas of the home as reminders that positive emotions are the powerful way to teach. Can also use "We-do" statements.

- Have parent select a routine to establish for self, baby, or family using the steps for setting up a pattern. Repeat the pattern until it is established.

- Ask parent to look for as many opportunities as he or she can to change a negative into a positive using SPE. Share what happens at the next home visit.

- Ask parent to select a toy available in the home and demonstrate how it can be used to teach the "Do's."

▲ Triangle Task ▼

Divide class into teams, or use other family members to help solve this task.

Directions: Here is a triangle that is equal in length on all sides.
<u>Draw three more lines</u> so that there will be
three or more equal sided triangles.

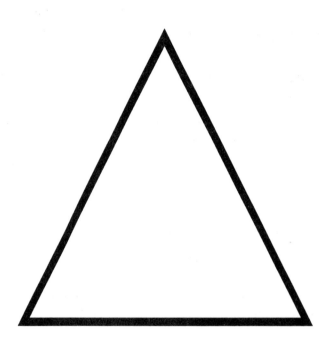

══ Triangle Task Questions ══

<u>Ask Parents</u>:

What did you think about the task?

Did your team share the rules? (three lines, equal sided triangles)

Did you or your team use trial and error, explore some options, draw some lines?

Did anyone quit? Why? Could a baby feel this way?

Did you consult together, feel a shared goal?

Did you use an adult or a book as a resource?

Did you share some fun with this task?

Did anyone think about a block ...
then draw the picture of a three dimensional triangular block?

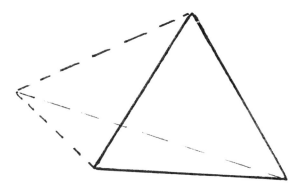

Teamwork requires learning the "do's."

Baby's Favorite Play

1. Describe a play activity your baby seems to enjoy.

2. What "do's and don'ts" is the baby learning from this activity?

3. When might these rules apply to other situations?

Playing Is Learning

A Pattern I Use

Select an activity for which you have a pattern or routine. For example: getting dressed in the morning, getting ready for school or home visitor, checking baby in at child care, going to the mall, preparing a meal, etc.

My Routine for _____

List or describe the steps you follow when doing this activity. What is the pattern or routine you use each time?

1.

2.

3.

4.

5.

6.

7.

8.

9.

10.

How or why did you develop this particular pattern for this activity?

What are the benefits of having this routine?

Building a Pattern Together

When you follow the same pattern for an activity, you help baby learn a routine. This becomes a habit. Most babies like to continue to follow the patterns you set. When babies have this structure, they like to show their mastery of it. They are easier for parents to care for and enjoy.

When babies do not have a pattern to follow, they become fussy and disorganized in their behavior. When parents are disorganized, babies are usually unhappy and confused. They are hard to care for.

Remember, even a 3-year-old is still a baby. You will need to support and scaffold all tasks. You will need to stabilize and regulate emotions. You will be providing the base for learning.

Identify a daily routine/pattern in which baby can join and be helpful: _____

(activity)

1. Define your needs (what do YOU need to have happen?):

2. How could you set the stage for this activity to be successful?

3. **Define the pattern:**

    a) what are developmentally appropriate expectations for your baby for this activity?

    b) what "do's" could you model for your baby?

    c) what are the specific steps or tasks for this activity that baby can help with?

        1.
        2.
        3.
        4.
        5.

4. Don't forget to ignore mistakes and to praise baby for following the routine.

    TRY THIS PATTERN WITH BABY AT LEAST 3 TIMES.

    Did baby seem to learn the pattern and to expect the next step?

The "Do's": Helping Baby Learn a Pattern

Setting patterns gives babies guidelines to follow.
In this way your baby will learn the behaviors you like by doing them with you.

At about one year, babies try to be independent. Letting babies try to do things themselves helps stabilize them. When you give them a pattern, they can often find success.

When you join-in with the baby, you can re-direct and reinforce the pattern.

Steps for setting patterns for babies:

• Do define your own needs. (*I need baby's teeth brushed.*)

• Do set the stage. (*Get a stool or box for baby to stand on; have tooth brush, wash rag and tooth paste ready.*)

• Do define the task.
   "It is time to brush your teeth."

• Do be clear ...We do this now.
   "We do use tooth paste."

• Do be consistent, follow the same pattern each time.
   "There's your tooth brush. Can you reach it?"

• Do be developmentally appropriate.
   "Can you brush each tooth? Good boy!"

• Do model the "do's."
   "Now my turn. I'll brush the rest."

• Do break the task into small steps.
   "Here's your cup. We do take a swish."

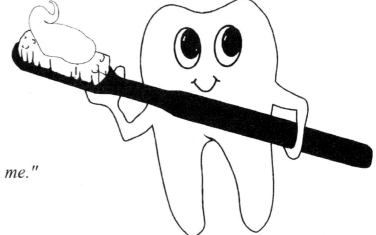

• Do ignore mistakes.
   "Spit it out. Oops! Like this. Watch me."

• Do praise the child.
   "Good boy! All done!"

The Power of Positive Emotions (SPE)

Emotion is the language of infancy.

      Babies communicate through emotional signals.

      Babies can understand emotional signals in others, from birth.

      Babies read parents' feelings through touch, voice, and face.

Babies tend to take on the emotions of their parents.

      By sharing their parents' feelings, they learn about the feelings of others.

      This is one way babies learn to fit in and belong.

      People have always understood one another more through feelings than
         by words or customs.

It is through sharing feelings that babies will develop empathy.

      Empathy is the ability to understand the feelings of another.

      Empathy is what allows us to have values and set standards
         of tolerance, courtesy, trust and respect.

Sharing Positive Emotions is different from sharing negative emotions.

      Positive emotions are processed differently in the brain.

      Sharing positive emotions (SPE) makes us feel close, accepted and valued.

      This is what gives stability and resiliency to a baby.

      Sharing negative emotions can be frightening or bring out anger.

      This can make a baby feel devalued and disorganized.

Parents set the foundation.

      By using laughter, surprise, interest, excitement, and joy in your voice
         and actions, you will be nurturing strong emotional development.

      By sharing times of contentment, loving, closeness, and comfort, you will be
         strengthening Baby's self-confidence.

      By using rhythm and music, memory traces are enhanced.

Keep more positive emotions than negative emotions in your baby's life.

      Sharing positives makes baby feel safe.

      Babies will then explore and learn more.

      They will mind better, be more cooperative.

      Parents are setting the pattern for future relationships and learning.

Feelings of confidence and Pride come from SPE.

Positive Emotions Propel Learning

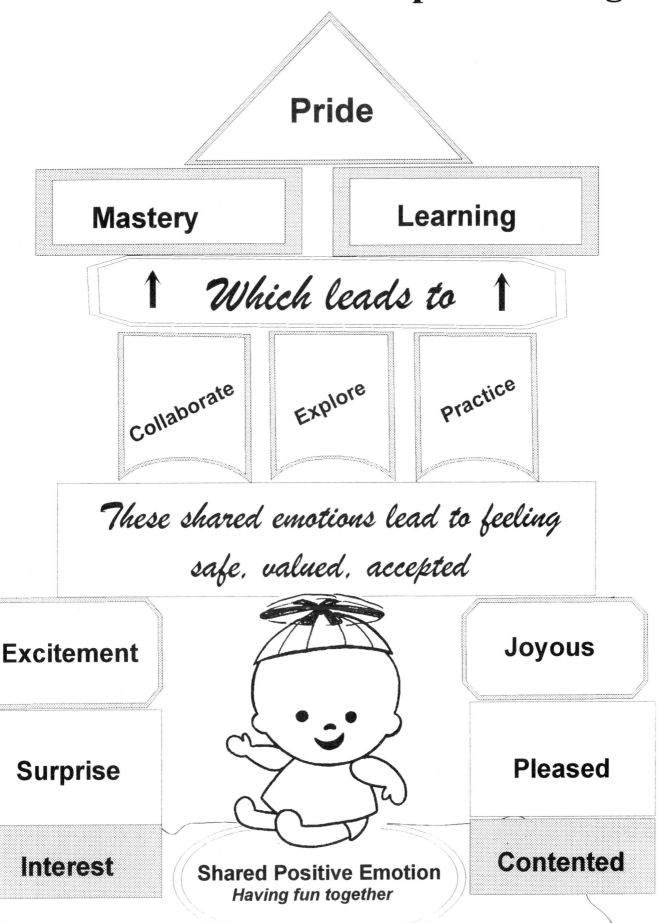

Pride

Mastery

Learning

↑ *Which leads to* ↑

Collaborate

Explore

Practice

These shared emotions lead to feeling safe, valued, accepted

Excitement

Joyous

Surprise

Pleased

Interest

Contented

Shared Positive Emotion
Having fun together

Positive Emotions Propel Learning

↑ *Which leads to* ↑

These shared emotions lead to feeling safe, valued, accepted

Shared Positive Emotion
Having fun together

Fun Can Regulate Behavior

With surprise, excitement, or interest we can help balance the baby who is becoming over frustrated, over focused, distracted, or oppositional. Distracting, or re-focusing, a toddler with positive emotions is a good tool for discipline.

Think of a time when you could have used **the power of surprise** to change baby's behavior.

Think of a time when you could have used **the power of laughter** to change baby's behavior.

Think of a time when you could have used **the power of excitement** to change baby's behavior.

Think of a time when you could have used **the power of praise** to change baby's behavior.

Think of a time when you could have used **the power of calm control** to change baby's behavior.

A+ Ideas for Teaching the "Do's"

1. **Do join in...use the "We" word...be a team with your baby.** When you and your baby are a "team," your baby will try harder to learn the do's. Babies view themselves as "one" with their parents; therefore using the word "we" is more convincing to a toddler than the word "you." Even when you will not be doing the task, use the word "we."
   "We are going to bed." "We do sit down to eat." "We are going to pick up."

2. **Do demonstrate what you want to happen.** Babies need to see their parents do what is wanted. Babies do <u>not</u> understand verbal explanations or orders. Parents need to <u>show</u> the action that they ask baby to do.
   Demonstrate patting the dog gently on the back by holding baby's hand to pat the dog.

3. **Do share positive emotions**. Sing songs about a task, make rhymes when doing an activity like brushing teeth or putting on p.j.'s. Make a rhyme about a task.
   "I put on a glove, you put on a glove, Honey, Ho, Ho, Ho."

4. **Do be clear and calm with negatives.** Teaching the "do's" involves also teaching the "don'ts." Negatives are strong teachers when they are clear and without emotion. A clear, calm "no," "watch out," or "stop" can alert baby to danger or caution baby to stop what he or she is doing. Clear, calm negatives are effective when they focus on the misdeed and <u>not</u> on the baby. Using the magic word "We" is also helpful when teaching the "don'ts."
   "No. We do <u>not</u> hit." "Look, here is a toy for us."

5. **Do use negatives sparingly.** When you have said "no," be sure your baby understands what you are meaning. Get baby's attention, repeat the "no" and explain why. Give baby a chance to change behavior, and then on the third "NO" <u>do something</u> about the problem.
   Quietly, clearly remove the baby, remove the object or change the action.

   Parents <u>never</u> need to use Anger with "don'ts." They just need to follow through. Baby needs to know that "Don'ts" have meaning by what happens next.

6. **Do keep expectations developmentally appropriate.** Babies will fail and become frustrated with activities they are not yet able to understand or to perform. New tasks are for exploration, experimentation and learning. If you want baby to mind or do something well, be sure the skill has been mastered before you expect performance.

Some of baby's objectionable behavior is a developmental stage, such as banging. This is a learning stage which will disappear on its own. You cannot teach a baby to stop a developmental step. You will need to be tolerant and patient. Developmental behaviors such as grabbing or banging will go away faster if you allow baby the opportunity to practice and master them.

7. **Do ignore behavior you don't like.** Babies will try everything to get your attention. They will repeat any behavior that you respond to. _It is No response that will extinguish the behavior_. Ignoring a "naughty" baby is a great tool for behavior management. Use it often.
"Let's go home now." Kevin runs away screaming "No-o-o-o" Parent ignores him, puts on own coat and talks to friend. Kevin comes back to parent, puts on his coat and they leave. The parent has ignored the baby's fuss and avoided the battle.

8. **Do divert baby.** Use rhythm, surprise, and interest to divert baby when baby gets bored, fussy, or is interested in something forbidden. Change the game. Change environment. Change the toys. Babies have a very short attention span. They are usually diverted easily, especially with excitement in your voice. No need to scold or call attention to your concerns.
"Baby takes candy off of grocery shelf. Parent says, "Look, here is a doggy. See the doggy on the box?" Hands baby a box of animal crackers, takes candy, moves on.

How do you describe a toddler?

As you read this description of a toddler below, fill in the ten blanks with these words.

challenge	exhausting	model
explorer	five	power
excitement	ignore	safe
		two's

Did you ever think about having a toddler before you had one? When you thought of having a baby, did you think about having a cuddly, "darling" to rock to sleep, or did you think of running ragged after a fearless _____1_____ ?

How do you describe a toddler? Some people say "they are cherubs," because they are cute and compelling. Some people say they are sweet and loving. Is this because they nestle close in our arms and put their soft heads on our shoulders? They often pat our faces and say "I love you."

Some people tell us toddlers are "clever." They can open any drawer or cupboard. Toddlers are often described as "busy." They can move very fast, but mostly they never stop moving. One of our leading professional football players followed a two-year-old around for one day and said it was more _____2_____ than training camp. Maybe this is why some parents describe toddlers as "into everything." They will find your make up, riffle your purse, lose your car keys, pull out the pans, dump the sugar, and spray water everywhere. Was "Dennis the Menace" a toddler?

Some tell us toddlers are "bossy." Toddlers do become willful. They_____3_____ rules they have minded before and shake their heads "no" when you correct them. This is the age of experimentation. Toddlers are experimenting with relationships as well as with household objects. The patterns parents have set in the first year seem to be lost. When parents say "no" to a toddler, the toddler may laugh and do it anyway. They are experimenting with "what happens if..." They are experimenting with their parents' emotions.

Toddlers are constantly testing their ___4___. "How do I affect my world?" "What are these rules for?" "Why can't I do whatever I want?" Toddlers are constantly testing their limits. How far can I go?" " How often will she say No?" "What if I cry?" "At what point do my parents give in?"

The toddler years are filled with confrontation. Toddlers' emotions are exploding. They are often "out of control" with_____5_____, sorrow, or rage. Did you know that toddlers need some kind of emotional stabilization from parents almost every ___6___ minutes of their waking day? No wonder toddlerhood is sometimes called "The Terrible ___7___"!

Toddlers try very hard to please. They want to master the rules. They most want the approval of their parents. They are as attached as they were in the womb, constantly looking to their parents as a ____8____. They are struggling to figure out how to stay in the "shared space" and also how to become independent. "How do I do it myself," and "How do I be like my parents?" "How do I find acceptance?"

Your toddler needs you. Toddlers need you to hold them close and give them balance. To model behaviors, to plan new experiences, to keep them ___9___ from harm. Toddlers need you to plan meals, expand learning, schedule the day. Toddlers need you for protection, to stay calm, redirect their errors, ___10___ their small mistakes. Toddlers need limits which are clear and consistent so that they can learn. They need discipline without anger and praise for each small victory. Your toddler needs you to share every task with joy, interest, and fun.

In a short time, your toddler will be three years old. You will feel very clever and very accomplished as a parent if you can make it through toddlerhood and have a child who loves to learn, loves to share, loves new people, new places, and feels valued by you. How will you describe your toddler then? As your "buddy"?!

Turning "Don'ts" Into "We Do's"

Use "we do" statements. Joining the baby always works better than "telling" the baby.

Instead of saying	I could say " We do ..."
1. Don't color on the table.	"We do ... color on the paper. " *and then* "Here, let me show you."
2. Don't touch the TV.	"We do _____ *and then* _____
3. Don't pound on the coffee table.	"We do _____ *and then* _____
4. Don't throw the rock.	"We do _____ *and then* _____
5. Don't step off the stairs.	"We do _____ *and then* _____
6. Don't pour out your milk.	"We do _____ *and then* _____
7. Don't splash water everywhere.	"We do _____ *and then* _____
8. Don't poke at the doggy.	"We do _____ *and then* _____

◆How Babies Learn the "Do's"◆

1. Describe a play activity which is helping your baby learn to socialize and to "fit-in" to your family team.

2. Explain how patterns/routines for an activity help baby learn the "Do's."

3. List 3 effective and essential techniques parents can use to help their children learn the "do's."

    a)

    b)

    c)

4. What are some of the special characteristics or needs of toddlers which make "teaching the do's and avoiding the don'ts" especially effective with this age child.

TOPIC 6

Roadblocks to Learning

Roadblocks to Learning

1. <u>Emotional communication can inhibit learning</u>. We have learned that positive emotions motivate babies to play, to practice, and to master skills. Sharing fun, making tasks into games, praising baby's actions encourage learning. Negative emotions have the opposite effect. Negative emotions alert us to stop, withdraw, and reevaluate what we are doing. Learning stops while babies respond to their anxious feelings and readjust their behavior. If the joy of discovery is thwarted, and if the pleasure of sharing is gone, learning is tedious and the feelings of mastery are taken away. Then there is no pride in learning.

2. <u>Negative emotions are like hazards in the road</u>. They stop progress and may cause a detour. Often when you avoid the hazard or take a detour, you never return to where you were going. When babies are faced with another's anger, fear, or sadness, they stop learning and begin another emotional process. They seek to escape from the extreme emotions of the other person. A baby's nervous system becomes disorganized as his or her thinking process becomes focused on survival.

Anger, fear or sadness from parents causes babies to withdraw and to wonder how to mend their crucial relationship with their parent. Babies then tend to feel angry or sad themselves. They feel unsure, off-balance. They have lost their focus. Learning can become paired with feelings of anxiety and defeat.

3. <u>Babies imitate the emotions they experience</u>. Babies who experience negative emotions often have more tantrums and more oppositional behavior. They can become devious and harmful to others, acting out their parents' anger or sadness in relationships with other people. Babies who live with lots of strong negative emotions begin to believe they are flawed people. They learn to feel ashamed and devalued. They withdraw from others and from learning.

4. <u>Anger is the biggest roadblock to learning</u>. Many parents have been raised with anger and believe that anger will be a strong teacher. The opposite is true. Anger frightens a baby. Survival is all baby can think about. Babies want to escape or fight. Some become hysterical. Sometimes it takes babies many hours to recover from their parents' anger and to be able to learn again. Often the bad dreams toddlers have are about parents' anger toward them or toward others they know.

5. <u>Learning to manage anger is a skill</u>. An understanding of *why* their anger is harmful can motivate parents to try to change their behavior. There are simple techniques which can help parents. The first of these, "Stop, take a big breath, ask "Why?" is often enough to refocus parents' thinking and quiet their fury.

6. <u>Teasing is another roadblock to learning</u>. Teasing is a way to convey dominance and anger by making someone else feel foolish. Teasing makes a baby feel helpless. They don't get a clear message, but they know that they are not OK. They are confused, off-balance. Over time, teasing may cause babies to distrust and dislike their parents. Teasing stops learning.

7. <u>Babies' own emotions can be roadblocks to learning</u>. Babies' emotional systems are as unschooled as their nervous systems. Emotions go out of control easily. Over stimulation, over excitement, exhaustion or fear can lead to hysteria. Often babies need help or coregulation from parents to regain their emotional and neurological balance.

At about one year, babies are able to remember more things, to dream, to imagine. Their minds can expand upon anger or fears which they have either experienced or witnessed. Then babies can easily become over anxious and out of control. Over stimulated or over anxious babies are struggling to regain their balance. They are not learning or hearing what parents are saying. They need to be held and feel protection and safety.

8. <u>Controlling anger is a green light</u>. All parents become frustrated and sometimes furious with their toddlers. Toddlers are constantly testing their power. They test every rule over and over; they try new things, get into parents' possessions, cry for help and need attention almost every five minutes. <u>Learning to say "No" without anger is the most important parenting skill parents will ever learn</u>. It is the most important gift they will give their babies.

9. <u>Setting limits with clear, calm, controlled messages gives babies a sense of structure and safety</u>. Making guidelines and patterns clear and understandable for the babies will give them confidence and teach them respect. Clear, Calm, Controlled Limits (we call them the Super "C's") are like caution signs. They tell babies to slow down, change directions, look for hazards. But the emotion is kept neutral. The shared experience is one of learning. This is why parents must follow through with their limits and take action. The desired shared understanding is one of "getting it right for the team." Clear, calm, controlled limits can give babies a sense of mastery and feelings of worth.

For parents, learning to reevaluate and redirect problem behavior and to reinforce the positive behaviors of their babies is a skill that will be rewarding for a lifetime.

•What influences babies' learning?
•Why are negative emotions roadblocks to learning?
•Why is teasing a roadblock to learning?
•Why can positive emotional extremes hinder learning?
•How do parents say "No" without anger?

Roadblocks to Learning

Outcomes:

1. Parents can summarize how negative emotions affect baby's learning.
2. Parents can explain how anger and teasing makes babies feel.
3. Parents will use clear, calm limits to redirect, refocus, and reinforce baby.
4. Parents will become aware of ways to control anger and other negative emotions.

Content and Concepts	Instructional Strategies for Parent Groups
INTRODUCTION: ❖Play makes learning fun. 　•If the joy of discovery is thwarted, learning can stop.	Display Instructor's Building Block #6 (see pg. 115) ◆Wordsplash Activity: "Play Propels Learning." (see instructions) Discuss how the Wordsplash activity allowed new ideas to be added to existing knowledge. What might be some roadblocks to learning?
•Losing the joy of learning can become a lifetime pattern and contribute to low self esteem and apathy.	Use Magna Systems Video: Play Explain how play and learning are intertwined. Discuss why it is important for babies to enjoy learning.
KEY CONCEPTS: ❖Emotional communication enhances or inhibits learning for babies. 　•Babies are motivated by the emotional expressions of others. 　•Positive emotions encourage and sustain learning. 　•Emotional extremes can inhibit learning.	Babies' learning is driven by positive emotions. ◆Illustrate using the "Road to Learning." (see instructions) Discuss how babies can become over stimulated by extremes of positive emotion.
❖Negative emotions are roadblocks to learning. 　•Strong negative emotions cause babies to focus on self protection, not learning.	◆Handout: "When Too Many Negative Emotions Surround Baby." Explain how negative emotions and emotional extremes hinder learning. Discuss "The Power of Negative Emotions." ◆To illustrate, use the "Road to Learning" with negative emotion road signs (car out of control, too bumpy, etc.).
•Anger is the biggest roadblock.	Now, place a rock blocking the road, to represent Anger. ◆Handout: "Anger." Explain how uncontrolled anger affects baby. ◆Discuss Handout: "A+ Ideas for Controlling Anger." Role play examples

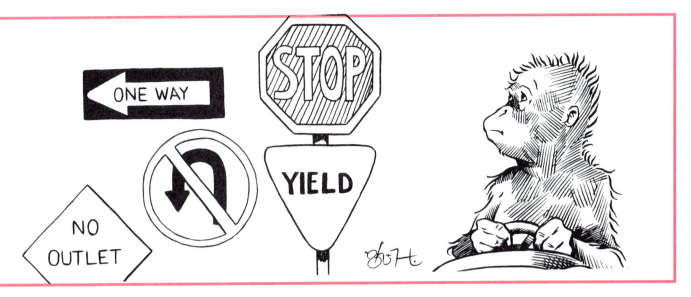

Instructional Strategies for Home Visitors

Terms to Understand

◆Wordsplash Activity: "Play Propels Learning" (see instructions)
Discuss how the Wordsplash activity allowed new ideas to be learned? Were there any roadblocks? Describe some road blocks to learning.

Discuss why it is important for babies to enjoy learning. Explain how play and learning are intertwined during the first three years.

Illustrate the positive emotions of play, using the "Road to Learning" (see instructions).
Discuss how extremes of positive emotion can overstimulate.

Explain how negative emotions hinder learning. Discuss "The Power of Negative Emotions."
◆Share: "When Too Many Negative Emotions Surround Baby."
◆Use the "Road to Learning" with negative emotions road signs (car out of control, too bumpy, etc.). Place a rock in the road, to represent anger.
◆Share: "Anger." Explain how uncontrolled anger affects baby.
◆Handout: "A+ Ideas for Controlling Anger." Discuss/ Role play examples.

Apathy
Lack of feeling or emotion

Defiant
Disregarding, resisting, challenging authority

Devalue
To reduce in value. To make a person feel small or worthless.

Emotional extremes
Emotions out of control; emotions overflowing

Foster
To promote growth and development

Isolate
To separate from others

Content and Concepts	Instructional Strategies for Parent Groups
❖Teasing stops learning. 　•Teasing is not fun for baby. 　It actually makes baby feel helpless, distrustful 　and angry.	Explain: the detrimental effects of teasing. Use "Road to Learning" reckless driving, etc. ◆Review handout: "Teasing." 　Ask parents to share their feelings about times when they have 　been teased. Identify ways people tease babies.
❖Clear, Calm Negatives used sparingly, 　provide structure, set limits, and allow 　babies to learn.	Controlled negative emotions can caution, alert, teach and provide safe limits for learning. Using the ◆"Super-C's" Transparency, discuss the use of clear, calm, controlled messages to set limits and take action.
❖Controlled limit setting is a skill. 　•It helps parents regulate baby. 　•It can help parents control their own lives.	Remove uncontrolled negative emotions from ◆"The Learning Road" and replace with Super-C signs. Discuss: How to set limits without anger. ◆Use "How To Say "NO" to Your Baby." Clear, calm, 　negatives, used sparingly, provide structure, set limits, 　and allow baby to learn.
❖Clear, Calm Controlled limit setting, 　followed by positives, gives baby a 　sense of worth.	◆Use "Redirecting, Re-evaluating, Reinforcing." Role- 　play several scenarios, in groups of two, using Super- 　C's ideas to set limits, ignore reactions, and re-direct 　to positives. 　Brainstorm when ignoring or walking away would set 　limits.

Demonstration:

Show how to redirect baby using shared positive emotions in any age-appropriate play activity. Show and comment on how you are using clear, calm, controlled limits to regulate baby's behavior (if needed) and to end the activity.

Evaluation/Closure

◆"Roadblocks Review: A Wordsplash" ◆"A Traffic Signal for Fun and Safe Play"	Parent creates a summary of the concepts presented in the "Roadblocks to Learning" Topic, using the words from the ◆"Roadblocks Review Wordsplash."

Explain: the detrimental effects of teasing.
Can use an example of driver scaring passengers by going too fast and driving recklessly as part of "Road to Learning" illustration.

◆Review handout: "Teasing."
Have parents share their feelings about times when they have been teased. Identify ways people tease babies.

Controlled Negative Emotions can caution, alert, teach and provide safe limits for learning.
◆Handout: "The Super-C's: Clear, Calm, Controlled Negative Emotions."

To illustrate controlled negative emotions, place Super-C signs on the "Road to Learning."
Discuss how controlled negative emotions set clear limits and avoid arguments.

◆Use "How To Say "NO" To Your Baby."

◆Use "Redirecting, Re-evaluating, Reinforcing." Discuss with Parent using clear, calm Super-C's to set limits, ignore reactions and re-direct to positives.
Practice with parent how and when to use Super-C's.
Brainstorm several scenarios where ignoring or walking away would set limits. How can we use limits to help baby feel worthy?

Limit
A boundary, an end point; something that defines an action

Over stimulation
When the environment is too much for the nervous system. Babies can't handle the sensory input.

Propel
To urge on; to motivate

Re-evaluate
To reconsider an action or idea

Reinforce
To strengthen by adding assistance or approval

Super-C's
Clear, calm, controlled expressions of displeasure; a good way to discipline

MATERIALS, SUPPLIES, & RESOURCES:

•Magna Systems video: Play

•Materials and supplies for "The Road to Learning" simulation (see instructions, this topic)

•VCR

•A rock, to illustrate anger in "The Road to Learning"

•Age-appropriate books for demonstration and interactive session

INTERACTIVE SESSION

Activity: Read a book to baby using SPE to spark baby's interest in the story. Use clear controlled limits to redirect behavior during the story. The goal of this activity is to keep baby regulated while reading the book.

Hints for Success

Some parents may not know how to express emotions when reading a story. They may need examples and practice.

Some do not know how to limit or say "no" in a clear, calm voice. They will need to practice using Super-C's and discussing actions to follow.

Videotape session if possible.

Set the Stage:

1. Choose an age-appropriate book to read to baby. Review or demonstrate ways parents can spark baby's interest in the book.

2. ◆Review "Redirect, Re-evaluate, Reinforce." Parent identifies 1 or 2 specific techniques for redirecting baby's behavior while keeping baby interested in the activity.

3. If parents haven't had experience reading to baby, they may experience some frustration. Discuss how baby's developmental level changes the task. Explain how to share a book in different ways to be "in-tune" with development.

Supervised Interaction in Home Visits or Parent Groups:

☆ 1. Using an age-appropriate book, practice keeping baby interested in the story while regulating the activity with redirection and refocusing behavior.
  2. See directions and procedures in the Introduction (page vii).

Closure:

Discuss how baby responded to the reading: What techniques seemed to spark baby's interest? What regulation or re-direction was needed? How was your behavior related to the baby's developmental stage? Review video with each parent, allowing parent to assess his or her actions.

Expansion/Enrichment:

Read often to baby using the techniques learned. Try the same techniques with other activities.

TOPIC ENHANCERS

TOPIC:
Roadblocks to Learning

For a Parent Group

1. Add topic poster, worksheets and information pages to parent's Play Portfolio.

2. Create bulletin board/poster: "Roadblocks to Learning" — use road signs to illustrate the concepts and the emotions which enhance or inhibit learning.

3. Post: "How To Say "NO" To Your Baby."

4. Display articles on the detrimental effects of teasing and uncontrolled emotional extremes.

5. Child care provider encourages parents to express positive emotions with babies during play.

6. Give each parent an age-appropriate book to read to baby at home. Or establish a lending library for parents. Parents could contribute one or two books (ones their babies have outgrown).

7. Discuss with parents how they might handle situations when they see other people tease babies.

For Parents at Home

• Observe parents and babies at the mall or grocery store. How does baby react when a parent yells or uses uncontrolled negative emotions? How does baby react to the use of positive emotions? Discuss with parent how he or she might handle situations when other people tease babies.

• Make a poster of ◆"Teasing Sends Confusing Signals."

• Make a "Road to Learning" book or game for baby. Use illustrations, bright colors, road signs, etc. Create a story about traveling somewhere. Use shared positive emotions to tell the story to baby.

• Toddlers' natural initiative and unschooled emotions cause them to challenge their parents' rules and limits. Use "DOOZYs" (see Appendix). Discuss with your home visitor solutions to each situation and any other behaviors which might be bothering you.

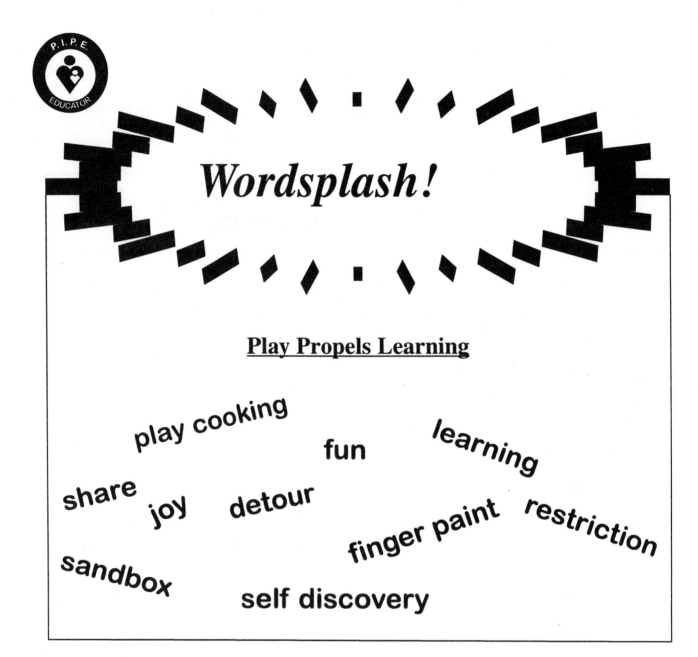

Wordsplash!

Play Propels Learning

play cooking

fun

learning

share   joy   detour

finger paint   restriction

sandbox

self discovery

Instructions:

What is a Wordsplash?
A "Wordsplash" is a collection of key words selected from an essay which students will be asked to read and discuss. These words serve to stimulate students to think ahead about a subject and examine their existing beliefs *before* they read the essay.

How to use a Wordsplash with parents...
In this lesson, distribute the Wordsplash above, and ask parents to write their own ideas about the statement "Play Propels Learning" using the words in the Wordsplash. When they are finished, distribute the essay "Play Propels Learning" and read it together. Pause after each paragraph or idea segment to discuss and integrate the parent's ideas. Are the ideas parents expressed, using the Wordsplash, similar or different from the essay? Did any parents change their ideas after reading the essay? Did thinking ahead and sharing ideas from each other expand their understanding of the essay?

— Play Propels Learning —

Play is a natural activity for children. They do it because it gives them pleasure and because it is fun. But, play is complex. An infant shaking a rattle or a little girl play cooking are having a great time, but they are also learning. They are discovering how the rattle works or what dishes are needed for play cooking. They are exploring new skills, discovering new information, and finding limits through their play. For example, some children will have fun squishing finger paint through their fingers and learning about texture. Others will discover delightful patterns that can be made with their hands. Still another child may discover how to create a new color by mixing two colors.

It is important to be sensitive to age differences in play. A three-year-old child might sit on the floor pretending he or she is driving a race car, shifting gears, roaring around curves and having a great time. A younger child might not play with the car at all.

Parents serve an important role in a child's play. Children will play spontaneously for a while, but they seem to have more fun when they can share the activity with someone. When a child plays alone in a sandbox, he or she often just scoops and pours the sand. When an adult joins in, expresses excitement, and begins to model new, creative ways to use the sand, the child's interest is increased. This shared experience motivates the child to continue the play and discover new ways to use the sand. As long as play is pleasurable, learning continues. If a parent gets angry or insists on controlling the play, the child's interest is decreased. The child may withdraw or look for something else to do. The joy of sharing, of learning, of self-discovery, and mastery have been lost. The child may give up the activity. The child may become hesitant to try other new activities. Learning will take a detour.

The Road to Learning

Instructions

   Use a child's Car/Road Set (or make your own using large tagboard) to represent "The Road to Learning." This Road should have curves, scenic views, bumpy road segments, cone zones, etc. Use a small car to travel on the road, illustratin babies' learning.

   Road signs depicting emotional communication will be placed on the road to illustrate the concept you are teaching. The concepts are: 1) how positive emotions enhance and sustain learning 2) how negative emotions and teasing become roadblocks, or inhibitors to learning, and 3) how controlled negative emotions give clear, helpful information.

   Cut the signs out and put pull-off tape on the back. Mount road signs to the "Road to Learning" at appropriate places to illustrate each concept. These different signs can be put on a flip chart or on several laminated tag boards and saved f subsequent use in several classes. Parents could assist in making the road and the signs.

MAKE THIS ACTIVITY AS IMAGINATIVE, ELABORATE AND CREATIVE AS YOUR TIME AND ENERGY ALLOW.

Road Signs for Explaining <u>S</u>hared <u>P</u>ositive <u>E</u>motions :

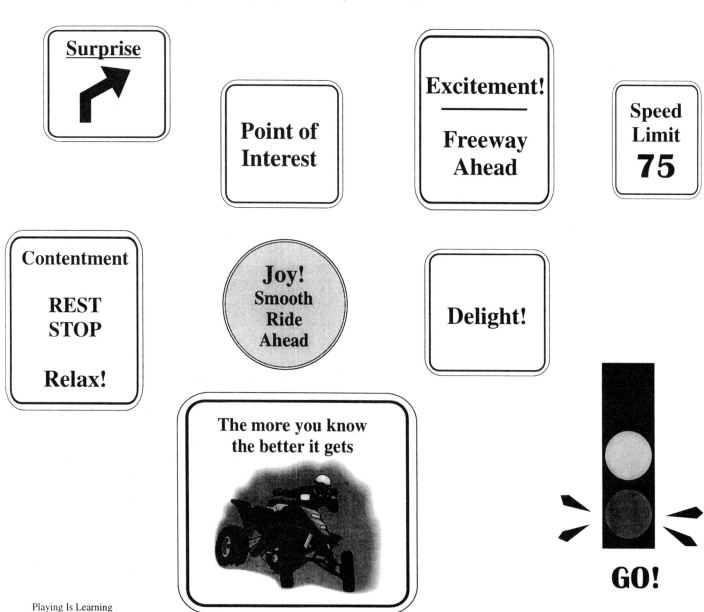

When Too Many Negative Emotions Surround Baby,

learning stops!

Road Signs for Explaining Underlined Uncontrolled Negative Emotions:

Driving too fast, out of control, on rough roads, etc.

WRONG WAY
Do not enter

Too
Fast

Out of
Control

STOP!

The Power of Negative Emotions

Negative emotions are powerful:

- They alert and caution us. We usually stop and pay attention.
- We usually remember them a long time.
- We work to eliminate negative emotions in another. We try to fix them.
- Babies are frightened by negative emotions.

Too many negative emotions are detrimental to baby:

- When there are too many negative emotions, or when they are too strong, babies withdraw and mistrust the person who is negative.
- Strong negatives make babies angry. They want to fight back.
- Strong negative emotions can make babies hysterical. They want to escape. They are not learning or minding.

Negative emotions affect relationships.

- When there are too many negative emotions, babies mistrust their parents.
- They become disorganized and unhappy.
- They often turn to others for a model.
- They often feel shame.

Babies learn from watching negative emotions in others.

- When parents model negatives, babies learn to act that way to others.
- They can become hostile and aggressive in school.
- They can become defiant and angry with their parents.

**Keep more positive than negative
emotions in your relationships.**

Anger Stops Learning

Baby becomes afraid.

Emotion takes over.

Baby wants to escape or fight.

Baby can become hysterical.

**Baby needs comfort
before learning can begin again.**

A+ Ideas for Controlling Anger

Take a Big Breath; ask "Why?"
  Why did baby do this?
Don't react.
  Say "I'm Really Angry." "I need to calm down."

Isolate Yourself.
  Walk across the room.
  Cover your face and breathe deeply.
  Put baby in a safe place so you can be alone.

Ask "Why am I angry?"
  Am I embarrassed? Am I too busy?
  Mad at my family or friends?
  Don't have my work done?

Ask "Why is baby acting this way?"
  Is baby tired, bored, hungry?
  Does baby need my attention?
  Is baby mastering a task, having fun?
  Is baby testing me?

Define a solution:
  Reorganize, Get help for my problem, Help baby with problem.

Act: Don't continue to repeat warnings or threats.
  Organize yourself, then get baby.
  Approach baby with love.
  Don't re-live the problem. Start fresh with something fun.

Don't model anger. Don't model tantrums.

Road Signs for Explaining Teasing:

Scaring passengers with swerving, reckless driving, wild turns, and power stops (see previous page)

Steep Dropoff
_____
No Guard rail

Reckless Driving

Teasing Sends Confusing Signals

Teasing is a mean way to convey dominance

Teasing makes baby feel helpless

Teasing brings out feelings of anger in baby

Teasing may cause distrust and dislike for others

Teasing stops learning

When others see an adult teasing a baby, they feel sorry for the baby and angry at the adult.

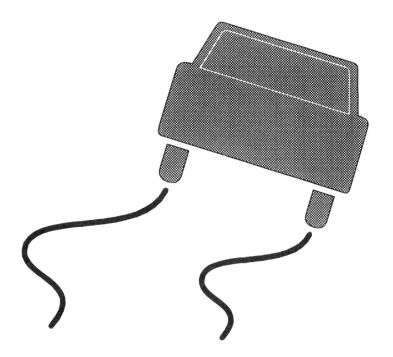

Road Signs for Explaining Clear, Calm, Controlling Limits:

Caution, alert, provide safety, inform. Drivers and passengers feel in-control and confident.

SLOW
———
Speed Bump Ahead

"We Don't"

"No, No"

"Stop!" "Danger"

Narrow Bridge

That hurts others!

Divided Highway Ends

Caution! Road Work Ahead

Reduce speed Wet pavement

EXIT RIGHT LANE ONLY

Share the Road

Yellow light- CAUTION!

DETOUR

EXIT ONLY

The Super C's
Clear, Calm Controlled Negative Emotions

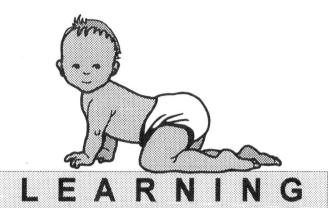

L E A R N I N G

They allow parents to reinforce positives.

They focus baby on "The Do's."

They caution baby to re-evaluate behavior.

| They Alert | They Protect | They Teach | They Set Limits |

Clear, Calm Controlled Negative Messages can be positive

♣ How To Say "NO" To Your Baby ♣

Get baby's attention. Include yourself in your statements.
"Michael, let's stop a minute. Look at me."

Calm the baby's emotions, touch baby gently.
"Come, let me hold you while we talk."

Give clear, calm messages.
"We don't throw clay. That might hurt someone. Don't throw."

Give baby choices.
"Here, pat the clay into a pancake. Or shall we play something else?"

Praise baby if it goes well.
"Good baby. You know what to do."

If problem recurs, Take Action!
"No. Don't throw. No!" Gently hold baby's hands.

Follow through with action.
Put clay away. Say nothing! or say "We don't throw clay."

Try to offer a new task.
"Here, help me put these spoons up."

Ignore tantrums.
Say nothing. Walk away and look away.

Always return to baby with love.
"I love you, baby. I don't like throwing clay, but I like you."

> Other ideas for action:
> •gently direct baby's hands or body to correct action
> •remove toy
> •remove baby
> •leave together (holding baby)

Refer to Chapter on "Love and Limits," <u>Love Is Layers of Sharing</u> text

Redirect....Re-evaluate....Reinforce

Helping a toddler learn the "do's and don'ts" of a relationship, a family or a society is a major job. Every few minutes your toddler will need redirecting. As a parent, you are constantly re-evaluating your toddler's behavior, and you are deciding how to reinforce the good and regulate the bad..

As a parent you are building on the strengths in your baby, ignoring and redirecting the problems.

• •

For example: Let's suppose Shelly wants to **redirect** Tommy.

She **evaluates** Tommy's mood. He has been playing hard, is restless, bored, and a bit whiny.

Shelly wants to **redirect** Tommy to a quieter activity.

Shelly says (with excitement), "Tommy, let's read a book. Look! This is about a Choo Choo! See, Whoo, Whoo says the Choo Choo."

She takes Tommy on her lap and begins to read. Tommy settles into her arms and becomes interested, pointing to the train and the engineer. Shelly reads.

Then Tommy starts trying to turn the pages beyond his mother's story and is tearing the book. Shelly takes action. She holds Tommy's hand and says, "No, no, don't tear the book."

Shelly **re-evaluates**. "<u>Why</u> is Tommy doing this?" ... Oh, I think he wants to go faster, to see what is next.

Shelly **redirects** Tommy. "Here's another book." Shelly stops reading the words and points to pictures instead. OK, Tommy, turn the page. Look, a duck! What does a duck say?"

Tommy quacks, turns the page, sees a cow and says "moo."

"Turn the page," says Shelly. Tommy sees a kitty and says "meow."

Shelly **reinforces** Tommy's good behavior. "Yes, a kitty and there's a little mouse. See. You're my good boy. ... "Turn the page. What's next?"

Roadblocks Review
A Wordsplash

Using these Wordsplash Words, make a summary of what you have learned about roadblocks to babies' learning.

•learning	•redirect	•ignore	•anger	•fun
•exhausted	•SPE	•limits	•teasing	•"no"
•modeling	•roadblocks	•caution	•controlled emotions	

A Traffic Signal for Fun and Safe Play

Directions:
Identify 3 emotions which
you think fit into each category.

RED LIGHT
Stop! These inhibit play and learning.

1.

2.

3.

YELLOW LIGHT
Caution! These can be used to alert, regulate, or set limits for baby.

1.

2.

3.

GREEN LIGHT
Go! These enhance play and learning for baby.
1.

2.

3.

TOPIC 7

Playing Stimulates the Senses

Playing Stimulates the Senses

1. <u>Babies first learn through their senses</u>. Touch, smell, sound, taste, and sight are what we call the senses. Sensory nerve receptors are the first pathways to develop in the brain. Babies feel motion and temperature in the womb. Babies also respond to sounds from outside the womb. At birth, all of the senses are active.

The senses become quickly refined after birth. By one month of age, babies recognize the smell of their mother's breast milk or their father's body. They recognize—through touch—the way familiar people pick them up, hold them, and put them down. They recognize voice, turning and calming more often to their parents' voices. Infants react quickly to temperature change, will calm to a rocking motion and quiet when swaddled securely as they were in the womb.

2. <u>Sensory learning is powerful</u>. Because all of our experience is sensory experience, the sensory pathways in the brain are very strong. Imagine a rope, connecting nerves to the brain: each sensory experience a baby receives adds a strand to the rope of recognition and learning. The "rope" becomes very strong, until the neuro-pattern of a skill does not require conscious thought. When we see a person, we don't stop to think about the effort our eyes go through to bring into focus and recognize the image. Walking, biking, and typing are sensory skills that become "non-conscious." Because the neuro-pathways are so strong, we <u>don't</u> forget them when we haven't used them. This is also true of familiar noises and odors.

3. <u>Play provides the opportunity to use many senses</u>. Playing different kinds of sensory games adds variety and balance to a baby's learning experience. It also may refine many skills such as fine and gross motor abilities or recognition of faces, sounds and odors. Some sensory games like learning a song together can make parent and baby feel close and enhance mutual understanding.

4. <u>Responses to sensory experience change with age</u>. A newborn may be very sensitive to light, but as a toddler this same baby is not bothered by lights. As babies grow, nerve endings will become insulated or myelinated; then babies are not as sensitive to stimulation. However, temperament will influence sensory reactions. For example, many babies, who were very sensitive to noise as small babies, retain this sensitivity throughout their toddler years. These are babies who have extra keen hearing receptors.

5. <u>Sensory experiences give immediate feelings of pleasure or pain</u>. This is why babies who are cold, hot, hungry, or over stimulated react quickly and strongly. When a baby or toddler is fussy or cranky, consider the sensory factors: temperature, hunger and thirst. A little food can change behavior remarkably ("How about some juice?"). So can a change of temperature ("Let's take off this hot sweater"). You can also stabilize a fussy baby who is too cold and doesn't know how to tell you. Parents act as co-regulators of sensory experience.

Experiences which bring fear send the strongest learning signals. Babies must trust parents to protect them from sounds that threaten them, smells that will sicken them, water that will burn their tender skin. Babies rely on their parents to provide sensory experiences which will protect, teach and please.

6. <u>Over stimulation of the senses blocks learning</u>. When the music is too loud or too fast, when the lights are flashing, when there are too many people, too many strange faces, too much touching and cuddling, babies often begin to cry and cannot stop. Their nerves are like fireworks, with too many nerve endings firing. This is a signal for parents to find a softly lit, quiet spot to help reorganize their babies ... hold them close, rock them gently and coo softly.

Under stimulation also inhibits learning. Babies who are left alone most of the time, who are never talked to, whose caregivers appear blank faced, emotionless, or very sad, have developmental lags. They begin to withdraw; they are not exploring, not experiencing new things. They are not learning.

Parents should provide sensory balance for babies. When sensory messages are too strong, too many, or become too disorganized, babies need help to regain stability. They need someone to steady and calm them. Parents do this for their babies. This is called co-regulation or mutual regulation. Like a kangaroo in its mother's pouch, when a baby's nerves become disorganized, the baby seeks to be "at one" with his or her parents. Sensory sharing is mutual, intimate, and special. It is the parent who can best rebalance the baby.

•How do babies learn through their senses?
•Why is sensory learning so powerful?
•Why is overstimulation a block to learning?
•How does development influence sensory learning?
•Why is play important in sensory learning?

Playing Stimulates the Senses

Outcomes:

1. Parents can describe sensory experience and its importance to learning.
2. Parents will practice age-appropriate sensory play with their babies.
3. Parents will evaluate how music is a sensory experience which can be soothing, stimulating, or dangerous.

Content and Concepts

INTRODUCTION:
❖Babies' first learning is through their senses.
- -Sound
- -Taste
- -Sight
- -Smell
- -Touch

KEY CONCEPTS:

❖Sensory learning is powerful.
- •Senses quickly become refined after birth.
- •Sensory experience directs baby's muscles and initiates development.

❖Play provides an opportunity to use many sensory connections.
- •Sensory play can balance learning.

- •Babies use senses to explore the environment and discover their impact on the world.

Instructional Strategies for Parent Groups

<u>Display Instructor's Building Block #7</u> (see pg. 141)

Candy Activity - Put blindfolds on parents, place assorted kinds of candy in small paper cups. Each parent has a different candy. Have parents try to determine what is in the cups - using all their senses, except sight.
<u>Discuss overhead</u>: ◆"How did you learn what was in the cup?"

◆<u>Review handout</u>: "The Senses."

◆Have parents fill out "Matching Senses" worksheet. (see answer key on next page)

<u>Sensory Rope exercise</u>. With five strands of colored yarn, or pipe cleaners, create a strong rope by braiding strands together. Discuss how each of the strands is one sensory experience which forms a nerve connection in the brain. These connections are called sensory pathways. Sensory experiences strengthen development and learning.
◆<u>Review</u>: "Brain Waves"

Explain how sensory play can balance development and increase learning.
◆Use Information Sheet: "Sensory Play Library."

<u>Show video</u>: <u>What Baby Can Do</u>. Parents Magazine, Volume 1.
◆Handout: "Sensory Experience for Baby."
Discuss: How babies are learning about objects.

Instructional Strategies for Home Visitors

Candy Activity - Bring small amounts of 3 kinds of candy to the visit. Select candies that have different shapes, textures, fragrances (e.g. bubble gum, licorice, lemon drops). Present each candy in a small paper cup or bag, inviting parent to be blindfolded and explore each candy without the aid of sight. Enjoy the candy and discuss how the parent learned what was in each cup. Discuss the importance of touch, taste and smell as ways babies learn throughout the first and second year.

◆Review with parent teaching aid: "The Senses." Discuss how and what baby learns from each of the senses. Have parent complete "Matching Senses."

Sensory Rope exercise. Use five different colored strands of yarn or pipe cleaners to twist or braid into a single rope. Discuss how each of the strands is one sensory experience. Many of these will strengthen the nervous system connections in the brain. These are called sensory pathways. They lead to development and learning.
◆Review: "Brain Waves."

Explain how sensory play can balance development and increase learning.
◆Use Information Sheet: "Sensory Play Library."

Show video: What Baby Can Do. Parents Magazine, Volume 1.
◆Handout: "Sensory Experience for Baby." Discuss: How are babies learning about objects?

Terms to Understand

Co-regulation
When one person can help calm the nerves or emotions of another

Equilibrium
A state of balance between conflicting influences

Fluctutations
Changes

Mutual
Shared; the same for two people

Neuron
A fundamental component of the nervous system that receives messages from the senses

Neuro-pathways
Bundles of nerves built up through experiences

"Oneness"
Shared emotions, shared understanding; a feeling of safety and closeness

Content and Concepts	**Instructional Strategies for Parent Groups**
❖ Development changes sensory responses.	Review baby's PDP. Discuss how development changes sensory play and learning.
❖ Sensory over stimulation or under stimulation influences learning.	◆ Discuss handout "Too Much, Not Enough, or Just Right?" Play various music selections with baby present (e.g. exciting, fast, vs. rhythmic, slow). This could be video taped earlier for discussion here. Have parents observe reactions on babies' faces and bodies using ◆"Sensory Sound Recording Sheet" (refer to Listen Unit text).
•Extreme stimulation is dangerous. -loud music -hot water -angry faces -rough or fast touch	
❖ Parents regulate sensory experiences and balance sensory extremes.	Discuss under/over stimulation and what parents can do to calm or stabilize sensory extremes. Use Information Sheet ◆"In the Pouch."
-Shared sensory experience co-regulates babies. •Motion •Rhythm •Singing •Touching	Observe or show video of caregivers rocking, singing, or touching babies to co-regulate them. Have parents list sensory experiences they like to use to calm their babies.

Demonstration:

Demonstrate reactions to different sensory experiences in a baby. If possible, show several babies. Use Cotton Massage and PIPE Activity cards.

Evaluation/Closure

◆ "Just Right Game"
   or
◆ "Play Is Stimulation of Senses" Review

KEY to "Matching Senses."
See previous page of teaching strategies.

A,C	E
E,F	D,B
E,D	D,B,A,E
D,E,F	B,D
B,D,E	C,A
E,F,D	A,B,D,E

Explore developmentally appropriate sensory activities for baby by filling out or reviewing your baby's PDP.
◆Discuss handout: "Sensory Experience for Baby."
◆Discuss handout: "Too Much, Not Enough, or Just Right?" Make a list of examples of understimulation, overstimulation and the right amount of stimulation you have seen in your baby.

Explore levels of stimulation in various forms.
Play music that is fast paced and chaotic, then soft and rhythmic music. Then use visual displays, with fabric that is colorful, rather than drab. Which was baby more interested in? more calmed by?

Make a list or discuss with parent what sensory experiences they create to calm their baby.
Identify techniques from "Teaching the Do's" (Topic 5) which involve sensory co-regulation.
Show segments from RYB Listen videotape to demonstrate co-regulation.
◆Discuss "In the Pouch."
Show a Madonna demonstrating co-regulation.
Review "Touching Techniques" (Love Topic 5)

Preference
First choice

Sensations
Nerve activation due to sensory experience

Sensory
Conveying energy from the senses to nerve centers in the brain

Sensory experience
When something stimulates one of the senses

Sensory learning
When the senses experience something often enough to remember it. When the nerve connections from the senses to the brain become strong.

Stimulate
To activate; send energy through the nerves to the brain

MATERIALS, SUPPLIES, & RESOURCES:

•Assorted candies: M&Ms, LifeSavers, Tootsie Rolls, Gummy Bears, etc.

•Blindfolds, small paper cups, overhead marker

•Parents Video Magazine: Baby Comes Home, Vol. 1

•Cotton or feather, supplies for massage

•Five strands of yarn, twine, or pipe cleaners

•VCR

•Video camera

•Tapes of different kinds of music

•Tape recorder

INTERACTIVE SESSION

Activity: Parents/Baby practice playing using sensory experiences, cotton massage, or PIPE Activity Cards. The goal of this activity is to show how shared sensory stimulation can calm babies or help babies to learn.

Hints for Success

Help parents select developmentally appropriate sensory activities which their babies will enjoy.

Monitor babies' reactions closely. Point out to parent when stimulation isn't pleasing or is not appropriate and how baby is showing this.

Videotape the session.

Set the Stage:

1. ◆Review "Sensory Library" and Activity Cards. Discuss how babies learn through their senses.

   Review the cotton massage technique. Discuss how to focus baby through sensory experience.

2. Encourage parents to select different kinds of sensory activities to expand and balance learning.

Supervised Interaction in Home Visits or Parent Groups:

☆ 1. Practice playing and regulating baby, with sensory experiences.
  2. See directions and procedures in the Introduction (page vii).

Closure:

Discuss: How did your baby react to today's activities? What did you learn about sensory experiences with your baby? How did applying what you know about your baby's development help? Complete a ◆"Face Check" for parent and one for baby (see Appendix).

Expansion/Enrichment:

Encourage parents to continue creating and practicing activities which enhance sensory development. Have parents document times when they regulate baby through sensory experiences.

TOPIC:
Playing Stimulates the Senses

For a Parent Group

1. Add topic poster, worksheets and information pages to parent's Play Portfolio.

2. Provide a variety of tactile materials - shaving cream on a mirror, play dough in the kitchen area, shredded paper, finger paints, feathery shawls in a dress-up box for parents and baby to play with.

3. Post on wall - Poster ◆"The Senses."

4. See Handout ◆"Sensory Play Library." Create other sensory experiences for your baby and share them with others.

5. Make a mobile which has pictures of an eye, a hand, a mouth, and an ear. Suspend it in baby's nursery.

For Parents at Home

•Each parent makes an age-appropriate sensory toy or book for his or her child.

•Using a sensory response recording sheet, record responses to different sensory stimuli, other than music, found at home.

•At different times of the day, take an inventory of sounds, smiles and sights in your home. Are there times when it gets wild? Times when it's too quiet? How does baby react?

•Observe baby's reactions to sensory stimulation when you are shopping or out with friends.

•Babies enjoy finding new sensory experiences for themselves. This can lead to behaviors which may annoy parents. Using "DOOZYs" (see Appendix) discuss with your home visitor ways to manage this.

How did you learn about what was in the cup?

1.

2.

3.

4.

5.

♦ The Senses ♦

♦TOUCH

Touching and being touched are different ways babies learn. Babies learn to know people by the way they are picked up, held, and put down. Touch can excite or calm. Touch can regulate behavioral extremes. Touch stimulates muscles. Touch is a way to explore and master new skills. Touch is a way babies learn about themselves.

♦SIGHT

Babies can see at birth. They see best at about 8 inches distance. This means that nursing babies can see Mother's face. This face becomes the most familiar image a baby has. Babies like to watch people, and they learn from the expressions on the faces they see.

♦HEARING

At birth babies will turn to the sound of a human voice. Rhythm and tone also seem to be understood. Babies alert, divert, smile, and relax to rhythmic speech. They also imitate cooing sounds and cry if sounds are loud and harsh.

♦TASTE

A newborn can distinguish sweet, sour and bitter tastes. By six months babies are beginning to eat some solid foods. Their likes and dislikes expand and will depend on parents' preferences and parents' faces and actions. Babies use the sense of taste to learn. They lick or bite most every new thing they touch.

♦SMELL

Newborns can identify their mother's breast milk by smell. They also respond to foul smells by crying. By being close to their parents' bodies, these unique bodily smells become comforting for baby.

and one more!

♦MOTION

Motion and rhythm calm and stabilize babies. Motion is called the vestibular sense. It is actually part of the ear. It is a balancing mechanism. In the womb, babies are moving gently and their vestibular sense is stimulated. They begin learning to gain balance or equilibrium through motion. Motion and rhythm remain a key way to get babies' attention and to calm them during the first three years.

Matching Senses to Learning

Match what a baby is learning about the environment through the sense(s).

A. Smell   D. Sight
B. Touch   E. Hear
C. Taste   F. Motion

_____ Mother's breast milk   _____ Voice fluctuations

_____ Lullabies   _____ A stranger

_____ Laughter   _____ Familiar people and things

_____ A pull toy   _____ Mom's sewing basket

_____ Music box bear   _____ Daddy's dinner

_____ A merry-go-round   _____ Where is my parent?

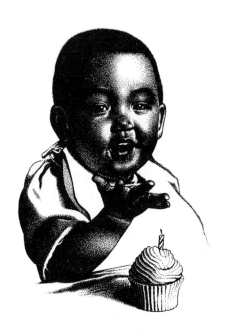

Brain Waves

Think about how amazing your brain is!

The senses	Your brain	Gives you action
Send a message. (You see, taste, hear, touch, smell, move.)	Checks your emotions, your motivation, your memory. Considers options; sets a plan.	It tells you how to feel It tells muscles what to do It stores experience in memory.

All information into the brain is sensory.   All learning begins with sensory experience.

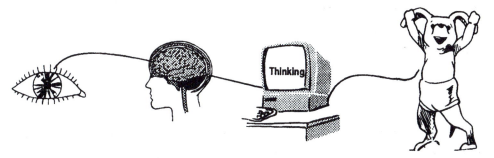

The baby's brain is brand new!!!

It can only process feelings and motivations. Sensory experiences create new nerve connections in the brain so memories can begin. Repeated experiences strengthen these connections. They become strong like a rope.

✳ **For baby, most sensory messages are informing new muscles.** They tell muscles how to move, stretch, grab. As experiences are stored in memory, choices occur. i.e., when baby's hand touches something, baby's new memory says "you did that before; you can either reach out or pull away." This is learning.

   For baby, most learning is about movement.   It is called Sensorimotor Learning. Each sensory message adds a strand to the nerves connected with memory. The connections become strong, and a developmental milestone occurs. With continued use, these connections become sensory pathways for motor actions. Learning is so strong, actions require little brain processing or energy.

✳ **People connect meaning to sensory experience.**
   This will be different for each baby because meaning comes from sensory experiences with people. Parents are the first to give meaning to baby's experiences. When baby touches something, one parent may say "pretty" while another says "no, no." Babies will understand experiences in a different way because of the relationships they experience.

✳ **Sensory sharing can calm and organize the brain for learning.**
   The brain needs equilibrium to organize and store sensory experiences. Babies become overwhelmed by too many sensory experiences. Parents can provide shared sensory experiences which calm baby and allow learning to happen.

See Piaget, sensory motor period in <u>Origins of Intelligence in Children</u>; Tronic on Emotional Availability (see Bibliography).

Sensory Play Library

- •Everything we learn is learned through the senses.
- •Babies do not have any experience or memory to draw on. They are making the first connections between sensory messages and muscle action. They need a library of experiences in order to learn and develop.
- •Babies cannot read or have a discussion; they learn by touching, listening, watching. They are also learning by smelling, tasting, and moving around.
- •Using all of the senses balances learning and development.
- •Play with another person adds meaning to sensory experience.
- •Babies will always choose to play with a person, especially a parent.
- •Parents can plan play activities which use all of the senses.

Play with sound:

1. <u>Change rhythm and tone</u>. Songs or rhymes get babies' attention; they give babies pleasure; they form a *together* feeling. 2. <u>Touch and sing games</u> ("wheels on the bus," ring-around-the rosie, etc.). Babies are usually focused and excited. 3. <u>Music</u> can alert and divert. It is an excellent way to change behavior or rebalance a baby's extremes of behavior. Lullabies relax babies and parents. They bring special loving patterns to mind.

Play with sight:

1. <u>Change face games</u> (wink several times, shut one eye and then the other, purse your lips, open your mouth wide in surprise. Smile and laugh with baby as you do this, so baby knows it is a game.
2. <u>Mirror games</u>. Touch baby's nose and then touch your nose. Put some rouge on baby's nose; then take it off. Put a hat on baby while he is watching in the mirror.
3. "<u>Where did it go?</u>" games. Let baby see you hide a small toy in your hand. Then let baby discover it. Let baby hide it from you. 4. <u>What'zt?</u> At one year, baby loves to be carried around to have you name objects.

Play with touch:
1. <u>Cotton massage</u>. Using different tactile stimulation (feather, finger, running fingers) trace baby's arms, hands, tummy and legs, feet and toes. 2. <u>Finger spreads</u>. With hand open, let baby grab your fingers. Then open and shut them and stop. Wait for baby to open them. You can surprise baby sometimes when he is in control. 3. <u>Blow on fingers game</u>. When baby reaches out for you, blow on baby's fingers or kiss baby's hand. Wait for baby's reaction. 4. <u>Clapping games</u>. Toddler will copy parent ... first in hand clapping, then pat table, then touch nose.

Play with taste:
1. <u>Different tastes</u>. Newborns will suck and swallow many different liquid flavors. But by three months, some babies will drink only their mother's breast milk. It is helpful to keep variety in taste. Serve water and diluted juice. 2. <u>Solid food</u>. As babies move to solid food, they often make a face and spit out any new flavor. Mixing the new with a beloved flavor and gradually switching the mix helps introduce a new taste. 3. <u>Experiment with taste</u>. Let toddlers taste what they want if it is safe; try the lemon, try the ice cream, taste the coffee, try the spaghetti. Parents can use fun emotional signals to express each flavor. In this way, babies learn what <u>you</u> think of a flavor. 4. <u>Safety cautions</u>: Babies will try to eat almost anything: soap, dirt, cleaning powder. When they are teething, they put everything in their mouths. Parents must put non-edible and poisonous things up high. Parents must also be vigilant so toddlers don't choke on small objects, blocks, doll's eyes, nuts, popcorn, hot dogs, balloons, etc.

Play with smell:
Babies have a good sense of smell very early in life. When parents are in the room, babies know this by smell. 1. <u>Share smells</u>. The six-month-old enjoys smelling flowers, the dog, your food, his own food. When you point out odors and express your feelings in a fun way, baby will learn to identify different smells. 2. <u>Set up "sniffy moments"</u> when you and baby share smell games. Try sniffing the stuff in the bathroom: soap, bubble bath, perfume, shampoo, or try the herb section at the grocery. Stop and smell thyme, rosemary, sage, lemon dill. <u>Caution</u>: Watch out for powders, chilies, sharp, foul smells. Some substances can be inhaled and choke baby.

Play with motion:
Motion seems to be special for babies. 1. <u>Rocking motion</u>: can soothe baby. 2. <u>Dancing</u>: Swaying and dipping with baby close to your body gives pleasure. 3. <u>Bouncing and bicycling games</u>, like "Wheels on the Bus," or "Ride a Cock Horse." 4. <u>Rhythm games</u>, like tapping on baby's foot or tummy. 5. <u>Chase games</u> for toddlers: "I'm gonna get you!" <u>Caution</u>: Jumping is an irresistible motion for toddlers. Watch so that your baby doesn't fall from a bed or chair.

Sensory Experiences for Baby

Skills/Objectives	Activities Which Enhance Development
1-3 mos. • Use eye muscles to focus on objects. • Baby is learning to recognize people and objects.	Take an enlarged photo, or interesting design and position it so the baby can see it. Move the photo to another location in the crib after a few days. Enlarged pictures of caregivers or family members may be used.
3-6 mos. • Develop reaching and grasping skills. • Baby is learning to discriminate objects by their sounds, looks, and feel.	Suspend a variety of objects from a sturdy twine tied between the top rails of the baby's crib. Objects such as a baby rattle, metal spoon, stuffed toy, small unbreakable mirror, glove, or bell are good choices. Change the objects frequently to maintain the baby's interest. (Do not leave infant unattended and remove twine and objects when play time is over.)
6-8 mos. • Encourage tactile sensory experience. • Baby is learning differences in objects through taste and visual experience.	Select a variety of objects with different textures for the baby to explore (stuffed toys, soft plastic toys with knobby textures, objects with smooth surfaces, rough terry cloth, velvet, etc.).
9-12 mos. • Practice using auditory and visual cues. • Babies are learning to locate objects they cannot see.	The parent hides behind an object such as a door or chair and uses an auditory cue "Come and get me!" A visual cue such as popping in and out of the hiding place can also assist the baby. Baby finds parent and gets a hug as a reward. When the interaction is gentle, friendly and warm, most babies will enjoy this activity.
12-15 mos. • Practice eye-hand coordination . • Baby is learning about the results of his actions on the things he is playing with.	Using water or edible materials, such as cream of wheat or cornmeal, allow babies to dump, fill, and pour. Collect a variety of utensils and containers for baby to explore, such as plastic scoops, squeeze bottles, and sand toys for playing in bath, sand pile, or on floor.

── Sound Response Recording Sheet ──

This form allows you to record your baby's responses to sound.
Complete this page recording all the cues you observe.
You may use more than one response for each item.

Observe baby's response cues: what does baby's body do, what do baby's eyes do, what does baby's head do, what does baby's voice do, etc.? What is baby saying?

My baby reacts to different kinds of music in these ways:

Type of music	What is baby saying?	Does music soothe, stimulate, frighten, or amaze baby?
Example: LOUD	Startles, cringes, turns away, grimaces	Amazed; fearful
SLOW		
FAST		
SOFT		
LULLABY		
ROCK		
CLASSICAL		
COUNTRY WESTERN		
JAZZ or RAP		

Too Much, Not Enough, Just Right

Too Much

Sensory experiences give immediate feelings of pleasure or pain. This is why babies who are over stimulated, too cold, too hot, or too hungry react quickly and strongly. Early signs of over stimulation are when babies look away or close their eyes. Other signs are hiccups, spitups, or sudden bowel movements.

When music is too loud, when lights are flashing or glaring, when there are too many people, too many strange faces, or even too much cuddling, babies often begin to cry and cannot stop. Their nerves are like fireworks, all firing at once.

Extreme tastes and extreme smells are too much for babies' sensitive pathways. Do not tease babies with these extremes.

Parents can help an over stimulated baby regain balance. Find a darkened, quiet spot to help baby reorganize. Parent's body, voice and face will steady baby. Then leave baby for some quiet time alone. Often toddlers prefer to be left alone in a safe, familiar place. They sometimes even ask for "time-out," just for this reason.

Not Enough

Under stimulation of the senses is also a roadblock to learning. Babies who are left alone most of the time, babies who have very sad parents, babies who are never talked to or played with become blank-faced and withdrawn. They do not explore. They often become frightened of new people and new things. These babies lose abilities to form relationships with others.

Just Right!

When parents are sensitive to their babies' responses, they can change stimulation as babies grow, e.g., the newborn who is sensitive to light soon learns to adapt to light and is no longer over stimulated by it. Sensitive parents are thinking about what is 'just right' for baby.

Hearing receptors in babies remain very sensitive. Loud sounds can actually damage babies' hearing. This is true for sounds outside, as well as inside.

Touch is tied to temperament. Some babies like to be cuddled a lot; others like some closeness, but then object to feeling confined. Some parents know that their babies would rather be put down when fussy than to be rocked.

Taste and Smell are closely related to what parents like. Babies raised in a house where the cooking odors are very spicy, where parent's perfumes are strong, where animals live in the corral, may be exposed to more variety in odors than other children.

"In the Pouch"

Co-regulation and Mutual regulation of the sensory system

❖ When sensory messages are too strong ... or too many ... or when the nervous system becomes disorganized ... babies need help to regain balance.
They need someone to steady and calm them. Parents do this for their babies.
This is called co-regulation. "*Together* we can find balance."

❖ Throughout nature, babies stay close to their parents. They do this to find food and protection. They do this because parents provide a model of behavior, and we also know that babies stay close because parents steady their nervous systems.

❖ Like the Kangaroo baby who can jump into Mama's pouch and feel "at one" with her, human babies also feel "at one" with their parents when they are in their arms, holding their hand or even just touching. Just seeing a parent across the room or hearing a parent's voice can calm and balance a baby.

It is this "shared space,"... this feeling of "oneness" that organizes sensory messages and regulates the nervous system.

❖ Very often parent and baby regulate one another.
The baby is calmed by the mother, and the mother is calmed by rocking and singing to her baby.
This is called mutual regulation.

❖ "Babies need to feel "at one" with their parent.
Like Baby Roo, "in the pouch" is where babies find balance.
"In the pouch" is where babies first begin to learn.

For the first three years, babies need to be able to "jump into the pouch," to feel a parent's touch whenever they feel off balance.

Where is your baby's" pouch"?

● **Cotton Massage Demonstration** ●
Refer to "Touch Techniques" in the <u>Love</u> Unit

1. Gather supplies - mat, cotton balls, feather or something soft, towel or receiving blanket. Take baby from child care center.

2. Select safe area for demonstration - a comfortable chair, couch, floor, changing table, table, bed. etc.

3. Use the Teaching Loop to initiate the activity. Tell baby you are going to rub his/her body with something soft. Continue talking to baby while you are gently, lightly touching his/her body with the cotton. Your voice should be soothing and comforting but continually changing in pitch.

4. Begin to slowly outline baby's body by starting at the head and working down the face - touching the ears, nose, etc. Continue around the neck to shoulders, arms, hands, torso, stomach, leg and foot and then go back up the other side. Watch baby's responses. If baby becomes tired or cranky, stop the activity. Be sensitive to baby's responses.

A nursery rhyme to say while you are doing the cotton massage is as follows:

> *Two little eyes to look around,*
> *Two little ears to hear a sound.*
> *One little nose to smell what's sweet,*
> *One little mouth that likes to eat.*
>
> Infant Massage, McClure, page 15

5. This gives the babies an opportunity to learn about their bodies through development of the senses.

6. What senses are being stimulated?

160

Just Right Game

How might these statement affect baby?

Rate the statements of parents below by considering the sensory stimulation their babies will feel. Put the # of the statement in the box you believe rates it correctly: too much, just right, or too little.

1. I like to listen to Hard Rock music.

2. I always test the baby's food on my wrist or touch it before I give it to the baby.

3. We pull the drapes and whisper when the baby is asleep.

4. Small babies need twice the clothes that adults do.

Just Right

Item Number

#2

_____

_____

_____

_____

Too Much

Item Number

1

_____

_____

_____

_____

5. My baby never needs shoes.

6. I tell my baby when I'm going to use the vacuum cleaner. We get ready for a big loud noise together.

7. The water temperature in our apartment is fairly even. I never bother testing it for baby's bath.

8. If I want to study, I just leave my baby alone in the back yard. It's fenced.

9. I show my baby how to smell flowers and foods that I like.

10. My 2 1/2 year old loves people. I make sure he is never alone.

11. I make sure my baby has a new toy every day. We never leave him alone. Someone is always interacting and teaching him.

12. When baby is babbling to her toys in bed, I wait to go in until she calls me.

Too Little

Item Number

3

_____

_____

_____

_____

Playing Stimulates the Senses Review

1. The senses are important to a baby's learning because ...

2. List four of the senses. For each sense, list one play activity which uses this sense to help baby learn.

3. What does sensory overstimulation cause a baby to do?

4. What kinds of music soothe a baby?

5. How can a parent use a sensory experience to change behavior when a baby is tuning out, fussing, or cranky?

TOPIC 8

Playing Is Imitation & Turn-Taking

Playing Is Imitation &Turn-Taking

1. Babies' first play is imitation. Mouthing, lip smacking, or tongue pointing—when imitated by parents—become a reciprocal game which brings smiles to a three-month-old. When parents smack their lips and then wait, the infant will copy them. This becomes a turn-taking game which both enjoy. Imitation leads to turn-taking; turn-taking becomes a pattern which baby learns and anticipates.

2. Babies learn from watching other humans. Babies are copying the actions, faces, and voices of the images they see and hear. This urge to imitate is another inborn motivator, one of the "voices inside our heads." Babies learn from other humans how to survive, how to fit-in and how to belong by copying. Even as adults we copy one another, wear the team shirt, buy what our friend has in the hope of belonging together, feeling close. Copying another's action is a powerful way to improve a skill or to learn the rules of the game.

3. Parents are usually the first model babies imitate. Babies copy their parents' faces, voice tones, and actions. What interests parents is what will interest their babies. How parents behave is what babies will echo. Parents model good and bad behavior. Babies cannot decide what to copy; they will copy negative emotions, anger, fear, sadness or boredom as well as the positive emotions of interest and fun. Parents' actions are teaching the "do's" and the "dont's" of behavior. They are modeling for their babies what they value in a relationship.

TV is often an early model for babies. The very young child is drawn to the flashing lights and then to the images. Many parents let their babies watch TV for long periods. These images stay with baby. Toddlers' fighting, hitting, kicking behaviors are often modeled after TV images. In addition, toddlers' bad dreams often come from TV images.

4. Imitation leads to turn-taking. When parents imitate their babies, the babies feel powerful. The sounds a four-month-old makes are experiments, voice play. When a parent imitates one of his or her baby's sounds, the baby knows his or her voice has meaning. The baby is thrilled and a turn-taking game develops. Babies strive to repeat these games and soon "a-a-a" becomes "da-da-da," and words develop. These early turn-taking games also set the pattern of *listen and answer*, which is part of learning language.

5. <u>As baby develops new skills, imitation changes</u>. As the baby grows, imitation will change. As the baby develops new skills, he or she will imitate parents, but at a different level. A four-month-old will reach for Mom's necklace and enjoy trying it on. A six-month-old will grab Dad's cup and take a sip. The nine-month-old will reach for Mom's pencil and try to write. The one-year-old will cry to use the big towel, try Dad's shoes, sit at the table instead of a high chair. Two- or three-year-olds will try to copy older children or other adults even if they have been scolded for doing so. They will often return when nobody is looking to copy something they have watched an older child or adult do. It is an important safety measure for parents to keep this in mind. A toddler may have been told not to use the scissors, the matches, or to ride his trike to the street, but if he sees an older person do this, the urge to imitate is almost irresistible.

6. <u>Pretend is an extension of imitation</u>. As babies gain memory, they will begin to practice what they have watched during the day. They can be heard babbling or laughing in their beds at night. When toddlers are alone, they will often re-live what was seen or heard during the day, scolding or loving stuffed animals. One-year-olds with toy dishes will pour and eat just like their parents do.

Pretending is a way babies can imitate situations and "try different endings." They can explore behaviors, acting out parts with positive and negative actions. It is a way to strengthen a learning pattern and master relationship skills. When the model is positive, babies strengthen good behavior; when the model is negative, babies copy and strengthen these actions.

Some one-year-olds seem to have bad dreams. They begin night waking once again, or they whimper in their sleep—reliving a scolding or frightening experience. Pretending is an important way babies integrate meaning into their experiences. Why were my parents cross? Was the wolf on TV really here? Parents are the co-regulators of these extreme memories. Babies can return to sleep peacefully when they know their parents are close and calm.

- •Why is imitation important to baby's learning?
- •Who is baby's first model?
- •Why is turn-taking important to language development?
- •How do imitation and turn-taking change as baby gets older?
- •When is imitation dangerous for a child?
- •How is pretending related to imitation?

Playing Is Imitation & Turn-Taking

Outcomes:

1. Parents will analyze imitation and turn-taking as forms of play which help babies learn.
2. Parents will practice imitation and turn-taking techniques with their babies.
3. Parents will recognize the importance of pretending and its relationship to imitation.

Content and Concepts	Instructional Strategies for Parent Groups
INTRODUCTION:	<u>Display Instructor's Building Block #8</u> (see pg. 163)
❖Imitation is baby's first play.	<u>Play an imitation game such as Simon Says</u>. Use examples of actions which babies might imitate: -sticking out tongue, cooing, hugging Teddy. <u>Explain</u> imitation as baby's first play.
•Babies are naturally imitative.	
•Parents are baby's first model.	<u>Parents identify times</u> when their babies imitated them. ◆Use Overhead: "What Does Imitation Mean To You?"
KEY CONCEPTS:	
❖Babies learn from imitation.	<u>Discuss</u> ways babies learn: watching, listening, imitating, exploring, experiencing.
•Through imitation, babies learn about their world and how to behave.	◆Using"A+ Ideas" discuss how imitation games lead to learning.
•Babies learn when you imitate them.	Discuss who else baby is likely to imitate (grandparents, child care staff, siblings, TV)
•Negative as well as positive emotions and actions are imitated by babies.	◆Complete "When I Frown..." worksheet. Discuss responses with parents. What are other negative models for baby to copy?
•Sometimes imitating adults can be dangerous for babies.	Discuss: When imitation and pretending are dangerous. Make a list of examples (such as lighting matches). What precautions can you take?

Instructional Strategies for Home Visitors	**Terms to Understand**
<u>Play "Simon Says"</u> doing things babies might imitate: -sticking out tongue, lifting arms to say "Sooooo Big," " Bye-Bye," hugging Teddy. Have fun playing the game. Involve other family members.	<u>Deferred Imitation</u> When a baby delays imitating an action, like waving bye, bye after Gramma is gone
<u>Explain</u> imitation as baby's first play. <u>Ask</u> parent to identify times when their baby imitated them. What does imitation mean to the parent? Use ◆"A+ Ideas" for appropriate kinds of imitation play.	<u>Imitate</u> To copy. To do the same action as someone else. <u>Irresistible</u> Especially attractive; impossible to leave alone.
<u>Discuss</u> ways babies learn: (watching, listening, imitating, exploring, experiencing). Discuss how imitation leads to learning. Who else is baby likely to imitate (grandparents, child care staff, siblings, TV) ◆Complete "When I Frown..." worksheet. Discuss responses with parents.	<u>Precautions</u> Care taken in advance; thinking ahead to avoid problems <u>Pretend</u> To make believe; to role-play voice and actions of another; to practice a situation in your mind; to act like another person.
<u>Discuss</u>: When imitation and pretending are dangerous. Make a list of examples. Discuss the need for precautions when baby is under someone else's care.	<u>Reciprocal</u> Shared, or returned in kind; each to the other

Content and Concepts	Instructional Strategies for Parent Groups
❖Imitation leads to turn-taking. 　•Turn-taking sets patterns of behavior, 　　and teaches rules and socialization.	Discuss how turn-taking sets patterns of behavior. Complete: ◆"It's My Turn" worksheet.
•Turn-taking keeps the game going.	Show Video segments from My Turn, Your Turn. Handout ◆"Steps to Turn-Taking" and review. Use yellow-sticky activity, from ◆"A+ Ideas," to demonstrate.
•Turn-taking is the foundation for language.	Discuss: how turn-taking helps language develop? Have parents examine PIPE Activity Cards. Identify activities which lead to language.
•Waiting time for imitation is individual 　　to each baby and is developmental. 　　-Sometimes babies imitate after a game is 　　over. This is called deferred imitation (e.g., 　　baby waves after Grandad has left).	Discuss how babies respond differently to imitation and turn-taking because of development. Demonstrate deferred imitation and other developmental differences in imitation using puppets. See ◆"Developmental Stages."
❖Pretend is a form of imitation. 　•By pretending, babies practice what they 　have watched during the day.	Pretending begins early in the second year, usually in the crib or when baby is playing alone. Identify times when you have observed babies pretending. Discuss how babies are imitating what they have seen. What kinds of toys encourage pretend?

Demonstration:

Demonstrate steps to turn-taking or imitation with a baby, using PIPE Activity Cards "Playing Is Imitation and Reciprocal Turn-Taking" #2, 5, 14, 15, 23, 24.

Evaluation/Closure

　◆"Imitation and Reciprocal Turn-Taking"
　Evaluation

♦When parents imitate baby, baby feels important. Start an imitation game by imitating baby and experience how this leads to turn-taking.

Explain how turn-taking teaches socialization. Parent identifies times when baby sets the social pattern (e.g. baby drops spoon from high chair, parent returns it, what happens next? Show Video or segments from My Turn, Your Turn. Review ♦"Steps to Turn-Taking & Imitation."
♦Complete "It's My Turn" with parent.

How does Turn-Taking help language develop?

♦Review "Developmental Stages."
Have parent pick an age and role play the baby's skill. Discuss how babies might respond differently at various times of the day as well as at different ages (e.g. alert vs drowsy).

Explain how pretend is a form of imitation. Identify times parent has heard or watched a toddler pretending.Discuss when pretend occurs (e.g. when in bed or when playing alone).

MATERIALS, SUPPLIES, & RESOURCES:

•Video, My Turn, Your Turn or Listen to Your Baby video, PIPE

•VCR

•Discoveries of Infancy: Cognitive Development and Learning

•Overhead markers, transparencies, small sticky-note pads

•PIPE Activity Cards

INTERACTIVE SESSION

Activity: Parents practice imitation and age-appropriate turn-taking activities with their babies. The goal is for parents to identify <u>their</u> baby's response time in an imitative or turn-taking task so that baby enjoys it.

Hints for Success

Have parents practice activities before playing with baby.

Monitor interactions to insure success for parent and baby.

Use puppets with older babies.

Videotape session.

Set the Stage:

1. Review imitation and turn-taking steps with parents.

2. Encourage parents to wait a longer than usual time for baby to copy them.

3. Remind parents to follow baby's lead, and not to be discouraged if baby wants to do his/her own thing. Sometimes imitation occurs when we are playing in other ways.

Supervised Interaction in Home Visits or Parent Groups:

☆ 1. Practice Imitation and Turn-Taking games with baby. Parents may invent their own activities. Use ◆"A+ Ideas" or Activity Cards.

2. See directions and procedures in the Introduction (page vii).

Closure:

Complete ◆"Checking What I Learned" (see Appendix).

Expansion/Enrichment:

Have parents write in journals about how they feel when their babies imitate what they do. Is the feeling different when they take turns with their babies?

TOPIC:
Playing Is Imitation and Turn-Taking

For a Parent Group

1. 1. Add topic poster, worksheets and information pages to parent's Play Portfolio.

2. Post the ◆"Imitation and Turn-Taking" steps on bulletin board.

3. Make a bulletin board which has examples of dangerous kinds of imitation, e.g. lighting matches, smoking, etc. Use the ⊘ symbol as a graphic element for this board.

4. Have parents observe in the child care center how babies imitate and take turns with the caregivers and with each other in unplanned activities.

5. Have parents observe when their babies are imitating others.

For Parents at Home

•Observe during the day, times when your baby imitates you or someone else.

•Parents make a list of times they played imitation and turn-taking games with their babies at home.

•Create games to play with babies which incorporate using imitation and turn-taking skills.

•Make puppets for activities.

•Include other family members in three-way turn-taking activities.

•The natural urge to imitate can lead a baby toward behaviors that are dangerous or that annoy their parents. Using "DOOZYs" (see Appendix), discuss with your home visitor ways to manage such behaviors.

What Does Imitation Mean to You?

What does *imitation* mean to you?

What does *turn-taking* mean to you?

A + Ideas for Imitation and Turn-Taking

Imitation and turn-taking start in the first three months of life.

❖ **2-4 mos.**	- Mouthing games, lip smacking, tongue pointing, kissing motions. - Cooing sounds, vowel tones — O, O, O; AH, AH, AH; IE, IE, IE.
❖ **4-6 mos.**	- Feet games: Gently push on baby's feet in a rhythm: two to the left, two to the right. Do this several times, then wait. Baby will begin to push back, wanting more. This becomes an expected pattern, a turn-taking game. - Reaching and hand games: When baby reaches out, kiss baby's hand. Then wait. Baby will begin to reach again for another kiss. You can make this a turn-taking game. - Sound games: When baby makes a sound you like, imitate it! Ma, Ma, Da, Da, Ba, Ba. When baby babbles, babble back. This is how language begins. - Eye blinks: Wink at baby slowly, several times. Or blink your eyes fast. Then stop and wait. Baby will imitate. Then you repeat. - Finger games: Give baby your open hand to grab. Move your fingers open and shut as baby holds on. Then stop. Baby will try to open & shut your hand.
❖ **7-12 mos.**	- Sticky Notes: Use small sticky note pad. Stick one paper on the baby. Baby will pull it off and stick it back on you. Great! Then try another. - Pat-a-Cake and Bye- Bye ... *of course!* - Blow on feet: Baby will ask for more. This is a good diapering game. - Sound games: read a book about animals and make animal noises. - Water games: pouring, filling up, etc. (can also use Cheerios)
❖ **12 mos. +**	- Baby will imitate everything you do.

Copying a model leads to following directions, focus, persistence, and feelings of mastery.

When I Frown

Respond to the following situations.
(suggestions: surprised, bored, excited, interested, etc.)

When I Frown, my baby ....

When I Smile, my baby ....

When I Laugh, my baby ....

When I Am Angry, my baby ....

When I Feel Sad, my baby ....

When I Am Unhappy, my baby ....

When I Am Loud, my baby ....

When I Am Interested, my baby ....

When I _____, my baby ...

When I _____, my baby ...

When I _____, my baby ...

It's My Turn

1. When my baby drops a spoon from the high chair, I ......

2. When I hand back the spoon, my baby ......

3. When it's my turn to talk and someone interrupts me, I ......

4. When my baby smiles at me, I ......

5. When I smile at my baby, he/she ......

6. When I don't copy what my baby does, he/she ......

7. When my baby copies what I do, I feel ......

8. When my friends ignore me, I ......

9. When I ignore my baby, he/she feels ......

10. Taking turns with my baby establishes ......

Steps to Imitation and Reciprocal Turn-Taking

Imitation

1. Start an action.

2. Talk about what you are doing.

3. Wait for Baby to think about it.

4. Praise Baby's attempts to imitate.

5. Repeat your action, wait.

Reciprocal Turn-Taking

1. Follow child's lead.

2. Keep it going.

3. Take it further.

Developmental Stages of Imitation
and Reciprocal Turn-Taking

1-3 months	Babies imitate facial expressions and cooing sounds. *Waiting for baby's response is important. It takes several demonstrations and a long waiting period for baby to start imitating.*
4-8 months	Babies practice many different sounds. Repeat the sounds which parents respond to. *Begin turn-taking with foot tapping, handing objects back and forth and rhythm games. Remember to wait a long time for baby's response.*
6-9 months	Babies begin imitating sounds and actions of others. They will imitate several actions in a row such as bye-bye or pat-a-cake. Sometimes baby imitates after the game is over (i.e. waves bye-bye after gramma's gone). *Don't scold. Join into the delayed game.*
10-15 months	Babies use toys to imitate actions seen around them: hug a dolly, drive the car, stir the pot, drink some tea. *When others are talking, expect baby to babble too. Babies imitate by joining the conversation.*
14-18 months	Babies begin to imitate what they have seen or heard when they are left alone, often in their cribs. They attach to an object (blanket or stuffed animal) which represents a favorite person and they will pretend and talk with this object. *Do not disturb this relationship.*
16-24 months	Babies like to copy adults when alone (like cooking, gardening, playing ball, reading books, etc.). They begin to play pretend games with others. *Keep some adult objects for baby to play with in a kitchen drawer or dresser.*
24-30 months	Babies demonstrate more complex imitation. They can copy a model such as a block structure. They act out different parts, taking turns with self. Pretend becomes a prominent game when alone or with others. *Parents can join in with puppets or stuffed animals.*
30-36 months	Babies like costumes - having imaginary friends. They set up pretend situations to re-live emotional tensions, or practice rules and routines. Babies continue to imitate what they see around them, trying adult activities like cutting, striking matches, pounding, cooking, walking alone, etc. *Parents should be vigilant.*

Imitation and Reciprocal Turn-Taking Evaluation

<u>Complete the following thoughts</u>:

1. Imitation is important to my baby because ....

2. My baby's first model is ....

3. The steps to imitation are ...

4. The steps to reciprocal turn-taking are ...

5. I like my baby to imitate me because ...

6. Pretending is like imitation because ...

7. At times it is dangerous for baby to imitate. Explain why.

8. This topic was important or fun to me and my baby because ...

TOPIC 9

Playing Is Communicating

Playing Is Communicating

1. <u>Communication is what connects us to one another</u>. It is the process of sharing feelings, needs, ideas and knowledge. All creatures communicate within their species. The porpoise, the elephant—even the starfish—can all share with others of their kind through a communication system. It is through communication that a species survives.

2. <u>Much of this is done through facial cues, eye contact, body language, and emotion-based sounds</u>. It is what is called nonverbal communication. The bear puffs up his fur, shows his teeth, and growls. There are no words, but the behaviors send clear messages. Many such nonverbal messages can be read by other animals and by humans because they are emotional signals which are similar across species. Behaviors can convey feelings.

As humans, we communicate feelings and needs with nonverbal behaviors. Our facial expressions, body movements, gestures and our emotional expressions tell others what we are feeling or needing. From birth, we can give and understand nonverbal cues. We continue to use nonverbal communication throughout our lives. Often the nonverbal cues tell us the most about one another and give us the clearest messages. Art, photography and music are also nonverbal communications which express feelings.

3. <u>Verbal communication is unique to humans</u>. Because we can learn words, we can communicate ideas and knowledge. Words connect us to the world of possibilities. Words allow us to share goals, fears and dreams. Through language we can negotiate, plan and inspire. Words allow us to write books, make laws, share poetry and song. Through words we are connected across families, communities and countries. Through words we can continue to learn and grow.

4. <u>Babies communicate through play</u>. From the first months of life, babies find pleasure in watching and listening to their caregivers. They soon try to imitate. Playful parents will also imitate their baby's actions and this becomes a game. Patterns for communication are set very early. Babies soon learn to listen and then respond to another's actions and sounds. Because nonverbal cues are inborn, babies can read them within the first few months of life. Babies will continue to read their parents' nonverbal cues even when they have learned to talk. When the feelings which parents convey with faces, voices, and touch are playful or loving, communication flows freely. When nonverbal cues are harsh or frightening, the baby will withdraw and communication stops.

Play helps babies learn words. With the use of words, the connections a baby can have with people, places and objects become an endless learning and sharing adventure. Parents are giving their children a gift when they talk and listen to them. Encouraging language development is how parents will give their babies an incredible opportunity for succeeding. Play starts first words. Encouraging word games, rhythm, and song are playful ways to teach first language.

Parents ... who talk to their small babies, tell babies what they are going to do, explain how things work, and give babies choices ... have babies who do better in school and in life. When parents learn how to listen and respond with relevance to babies' communications, they have babies who begin to feel mastery with words. As toddlers, these babies will try using words to express needs as well as feelings. When parent and baby connect in this way, they are sharing fun, sharing goals, and responding to each other openly. When both feelings and the ideas are shared within a communication, it is a special moment of sharing.

5. There are rules for good communication. It is helpful to understand the mechanics of successful communication. Learning how to give clear messages, how to connect with the listener, how to listen and respond with relevance are special skills.

Relevance is key to responding to baby's communication. Often we respond to a communication in meaningless ways. The message sent is not answered. If a toddler says "drink?" and parent answers, "I'm busy," toddlers will feel misunderstood. They will persist in a more urgent way to say I'm thirsty. They may fuss. They may throw their glass. Sometimes parents respond to baby with what is on their own mind rather than what the baby is saying. For example, toddler, ""Look, big truck!" ... Parents, "You spilled on your shirt." Relevance means responding to the message sent. For example: Toddler, "Look, big truck!"; Parent, "Yes, Big Truck, Rumm-m-m."

6. Reading to babies promotes good language development. Books open the world of knowledge and ideas to babies. Books can take babies exploring, or they can review familiar things which reinforce babies' learning. Books provide a way to be quiet and focus babies. Books provide a way for parents to share fun with babies. Reading to babies is a powerful way to play and to learn.

•How do babies understand our communications?
•Why are nonverbal communications important?
•How does play teach communication?
•What are the rules of good communication?
•Why does good communciation strengthen relationships?

Playing Is Communicating

Outcomes:
1. Parents will recognize that babies begin communicating at birth by giving and receiving nonverbal cues.
2. Parents will be able to synthesize the components of good communication and use them when interacting with baby.
3. Parents will analyze how play helps babies develop communication skills and learn language.

Content and Concepts

INTRODUCTION:

❖ Communicating is a process of sharing our feelings, needs, ideas and knowledge.

• There are many ways to communicate.

• Feelings and needs are most often communicated using nonverbal cues.

• Ideas and knowledge are most often communicated with words.

KEY CONCEPTS:

❖ Good communication requires skill and knowledge.

• Playing together helps establish good connections between parent and baby.

• There are barriers to communication.

Instructional Strategies for Parent Groups

Display Instructor's Building Block #9 (see pg. 179)

How do we define communicating?
♦ Discuss "Communication Basics," using the Key. Prepare statements, some which express a feeling or a need, (I'm choking, I love you, I'm cold) and others which express an idea (I prefer cherry, vitamins are good for you, etc.). Have each parent communicate one of these to the group *without* using words. Ask, "Did you learn more about feelings, needs, or ideas?"

Now have parents add words to their same statement and communicate it again. What did language add? (Knowledge and ideas?)
♦ Complete "Ways We Communicate." Discuss verbal and nonverbal communication and how each allows us to connect with others.

Explain: "A Communication Model." Discuss how good communication leads to sharing a feeling and/or an idea. The skill is in making a connection with another person.

Examine PIPE activity cards, "Playing Is Communicating." How do these play activities lead to a connection with a baby?

♦ Review or role play "Barriers to Communication."
♦ Complete worksheet: "Is This Communicating?"

Instructional Strategies for Home Visitors

Terms to Understand

How do we define communicating?
◆ Share "Communication Basics"
  Discuss and refer to the Key.
  Prepare ahead, statements which express a feeling, need, or idea, (I'm sleepy, Exercise is healthy, I'm afraid.") Try to communicate them to each other without using words. Was it easier to decipher feelings or ideas?"

Using the same statements, communicate them by adding words. What did language add?
Discuss verbal and nonverbal communication, and how both enhance communication, using ◆ "Ways We Communicate."

◆ Explain: "A Communication Model."

Examine a PIPE Activity card, from "Playing Is Communicating." How is this play activity related to the model communication process?

◆ Discuss "Barriers to Communication."
  Complete worksheet ◆ "Is This Communicating?"

Barrier
Something that impedes or blocks passage; in this context, blocking communication

Diversion
Something that changes attention; distracting; changing the subject

Nonverbal
Not using language; communicating with face, body, and emotional signals

Oral development
Relating to the mouth; developmental milestones like sucking, smiling, mouth movements, sounds and words

Content and Concepts	**Instructional Strategies for Parent Groups**
❖Babies communicate without words.	Discuss ways babies communicate (see Listen Topics 1&3)
•Babies communicate from birth using emotional signals and actions.	◆Complete "What Is My Baby Saying?" Discuss how babies might be feeling and how adults might respond.
•Toddlers mostly use nonverbal communication even when they can talk.	Watch segments from PIPE videos (Listen and Love) with the sound off. Observe and refer to
•Babies read parents' nonverbal cues more than words.	◆Communication Model to analyze how babies send messages, was a connection made, how did caregivers respond. What is meant by the maxim, "actions speak louder than words"?
❖Play helps babies learn language.	Show Video: Talking from Infancy - How to Nurture and Cultivate Early Language.
•Play starts babies on first words.	◆ Handout: " Making Connections." Brainstorm games which lead to first words.
•Parents who talk to their babies have children who do better in school.	Practice ways parents talk to babies, such as explaining situations, giving choices and recalling positive behavior.
•Finger plays are a fun link to language.	◆Handout "Finger Plays for Baby." Demonstrate finger play activities. Parents learn and practice finger plays. Discuss how they link verbal and nonverbal communication.
❖Play with books is communicating.	Discuss how books teach language, share ideas and help to regulate behavior.
•Reading to baby promotes good language.	◆Review "A+ Ideas for Reading to Baby."
•Books convey ideas and knowledge to baby.	
•Reading to baby is a good way to regulate behavior.	

Demonstration:

Use finger plays or PIPE Activity Cards to demonstrate communicating with baby.
PIPE Activity Cards "Play Is Communicating" #5, 6, 14, 17, 22, 24.

Evaluation/Closure

❖Complete

◆"Communication Review"

or ◆"Communication Word Search"

Instructional Strategies for Home Visitors	Terms to Understand, cont.
Discuss ways babies communicate. ♦Together, complete "What Is Baby Saying?" Discuss what babies might be feeling and how they are communicating. Refer to Listen Unit, Topics 1 & 3. Watch segments from the Love video, with the sound off. Discuss what the toddlers are feeling and how they show it. How do the adults respond? ♦Use "Communication Model" to analyze message sent, connection made. Discuss the maxim "It isn't what you say, it's what you do." Show segments from the Listen video with sound off. Identify what each parent is communicating to baby. How does the baby respond? Discuss how babies might learn language through play. Brainstorm ways play leads to first words. Try out a few finger play games with baby. Is baby listening? receiving? responding? Discuss how play with books teaches language, shares ideas, and helps to establish a communication pattern between parent and baby. Review ♦"A+ Ideas for Reading to Baby."	Prejudice A preconceived judgment or opinion without knowledge or understanding of the person, idea, or situation involved Relevance Pertaining to the needs of the user or the subject being considered. Satisfying another by answering a question or reponding to his or her request. Meaningful communication Species A class or group having common attributes and defined by a common name Unique Being the only one; being without equal Verbal Relating to or consisting of words

MATERIALS, SUPPLIES, & RESOURCES:

- PIPE Video Listen to Your Baby or Love Is Layers of Sharing

- Video - Talking from Infancy-
  How to Nurture and Cultivate Early Language

- VCR

- Video camera

- Overhead transparenices

- Overhead markers

INTERACTIVE SESSION

Activity: Parents practice finger plays or activities with baby which will enhance communication. The goal of this activity is for parents to identify the messages and responses they and their babies send and receive during play.

Hints for Success

Parents should practice some of the finger plays before playing with their babies.

Choose finger plays which are age-appropriate for baby.

Videotape the session.

Set the Stage:

1. ◆Review "A Communication Model" and "Barriers to Communication" with parents.

2. Identify and learn finger plays to be used. The activity will be more successful if parents have memorized the selected finger plays.

3. Discuss relevance: what message is being sent? Are parents responding to baby's cues? Are they making connections?

Supervised Interaction in Home Visits or Parent Groups:

☆1. Using finger plays or PIPE Activity Cards- <u>Play Is Communicating</u>, parents practice communication skills through finger plays or other activities with baby.

2. See directions and procedures in the Introduction (page vii).

Closure:

Parents review their own video-taped session and analyze using ◆"A Communication Model." Discuss any barriers.

Expansion/Enrichment:

Record and discuss with parents how babies responded to communication activities. Fill out, review and update ◆"PDP" from Topic 2.

TOPIC:

Playing Is Communicating

For a Parent Group

1. Add topic poster, worksheets and information pages to parent's Play Portfolio.

2. Create nursery rhymes and finger plays.

3. Post finger plays and rhymes on bulletin board or walls.

4. Find tapes of favorite finger plays and use them with baby.

5. Make an age-appropriate book for baby.

6. Go to library and learn to use resources and references to children's games (e.g. Sarah Williams and Ian Beck books, The Rocking Horse Books, etc.).

For Parents at Home

•Practice communicating using finger plays at home.

•Observe baby's nonverbal communication signals. Can you define what baby is saying?

•Reflection and possible journal topics:
  -What other activities do you do with baby that help communication?
  -Who gives the clearest messages in your family? Are they positive or negative?
  -How might you connect with others in your family?
  -List people you have "connected with." What was the situation? Did you share
   feelings and ideas?

•Discuss how communication problems can lead babies toward behaviors which parents
  don't like. Using "DOOZYs" (see Appendix) discuss with home visitor and/or other
  caregivers ways to avoid these problems.

Communication Basics

1. Communicating is ...?

2. Good communication occurs when?

3. Poor communicating occurs when?

Communication Basics

Key

1. Communicating is ...?

Communicating is sharing our feelings, needs, ideas, and knowledge with another person. <u>It is about shared understanding</u>.

2. Good communication occurs when?

When a connection is made with another person. When there is mutual sharing of feelings, goals, or ideas. When there is mutual understanding of one person's feelings or needs. The listener must be motivated to hear the message and to respond to the sender. This is where collaborations and negotiations begin. <u>This is where shared understanding begins</u>.

3. Poor communicating occurs when?

When the message is not clear or the listener is not hearing or understanding the message. There are many "roadblocks" to good communication. If the message is unclear, ambiguous, or off target, shared understanding does not occur.

Talking to one another is not always communicating. If the listener is not ready to listen or does not want to listen, or can't hear or understand the message, a connection is not made. <u>Shared understanding does not occur</u>.

Ways We Communicate

Instructions: Circle all the words that represent <u>nonverbal</u> forms of communication.

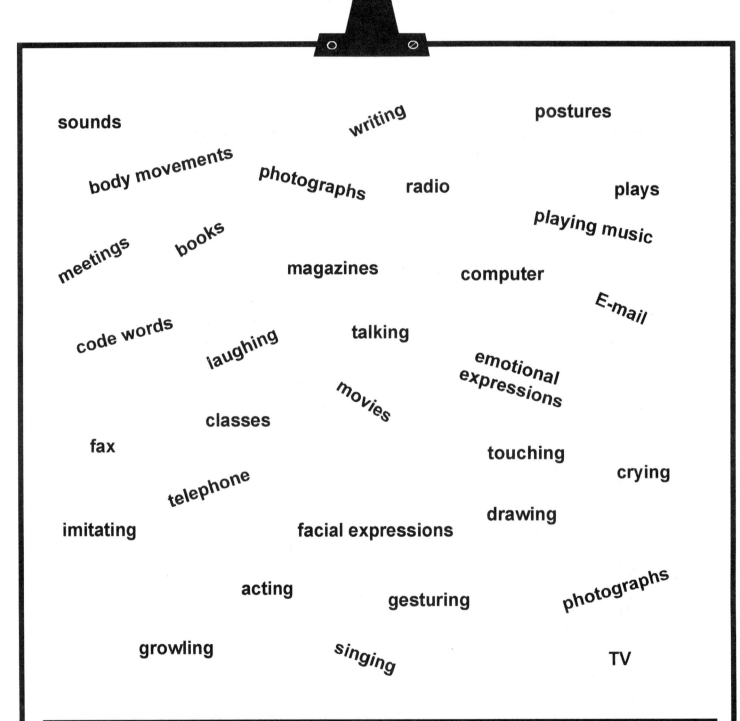

sounds

writing

postures

body movements

photographs

radio

plays

meetings

books

playing music

magazines

computer

E-mail

code words

talking

laughing

emotional expressions

movies

classes

fax

touching

crying

telephone

drawing

imitating

facial expressions

acting

gesturing

photographs

growling

singing

TV

A Communication Model

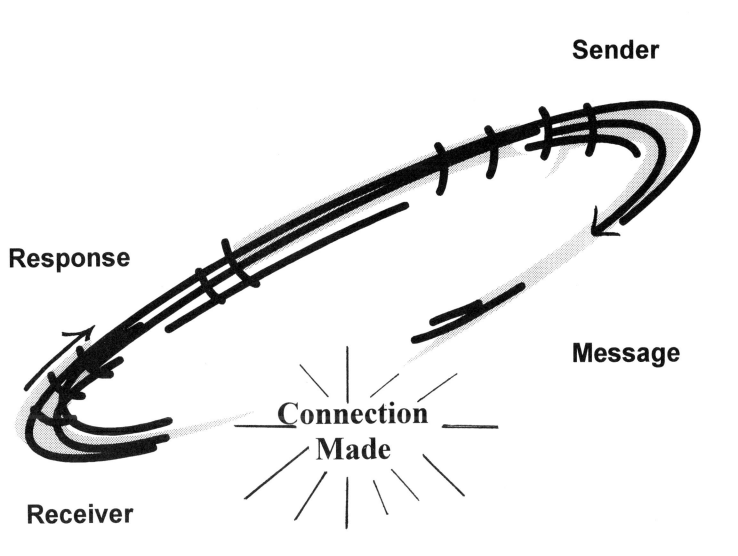

Sender

Response

Message

Connection Made

Receiver

Is This Communicating?

For each of the following situations: 1. circle the (sender) 2. place a box around the [receiver] 3. underline the <u>connection</u> *or* place an X on the ~~barrier~~.

1. A young girl is standing on the shoulder of a busy interstate highway. She sticks out her thumb. Cars whiz by her.

   What is the message?   Did the sender connect? Why?
   Is this a feeling/need message?   Is this an info./idea message?

2. Mom: "Where were you?"
   Jerry: "At Karen's working on a project."
   Mom: "Couldn't you have called?"
   Jerry: "Aw, Mom!"

   What is the message?   Did the sender connect? Why?
   Is this a feeling/need message?   Is this an info./idea message?

3. Toddler: "More drink." Parent: "I'm busy."

   What is the message?   Did the sender connect? Why?
   Is this a feeling/need message?   Is this an info./idea message?

4. Toddler: "Look, truck!" Parent: "Yes! Big truck, Rummm, Rummm."

   What is the message?   Did the sender connect? Why?
   Is this a feeling/need message?   Is this an info./idea message?

5. Parent: "Climb into your chair.
   Toddler: "No! No chair!"
   Parent: Baby, look we're having applesauce."
   Toddler: "Applesauce, OK."

   What is the message?   Did the sender connect? Why?
   Is there a feeling message?   Is there an idea message?

Barriers to Communication

*When Communication
Doesn't Work*

1. <u>The Sender:</u>

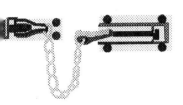

Tone of voice
("Uh-oh. Sounds bad. Do I need to escape?")
Body language
(Head down, arms folded; I won't like this message.)
Facial expressions
(What a mean look! I feel very anxious.)
Slang or big words
(What does that mean? I'll just ignore it.)
Prejudice
(He thinks I can't do this; how can I change his mind?)

2. <u>The Receiver:</u>

Noise, diversion, interference
("There is laughter in the hallway that's
more interesting.")
State of Awareness
("I'm sleepy, hungry, bored, anxious, excited.")
Past Experience
("Nag, nag, nag ... this is all this person does!")
Mood
("I'm watching TV. I don't want to listen.")
Health
("My ears hurt; I can't hear you.")
Prejudice
("This is not my parent; I don't have to listen.")

❖ What Is My Baby Saying? ❖

Babies are telling us things through their actions. Describe what you think a baby is saying when he or she does the following:

1. Sucks thumb —

2. Kicks at dog or toys —

3. Cuddles head on my shoulder —

4. Throws food on floor —

5. Screams and kicks when told "No" —

6. Lifts arms when I come into the room —

7. Falls asleep on the floor —

8. Plays contentedly by himself/herself —

Making Connections

1. Limit your own talking, especially questions. Pause often enough to encourage the baby to say something or take a turn.

2. Watch for and encourage any form of communication your baby uses (eye gaze, point, shrug, word, etc.).

3. Imitate baby's actions using sounds and interest words to comment on baby's actions.

4. Communicating to a baby is a skill. Sender needs to listen to baby, observe baby's state of awareness, and be on baby's level developmentally.

5. Let babies choose the objects or activities for play. Be prepared to watch and interact/comment on toys when the baby shows interest.

6. Include another adult or child in play. Be sure baby has a chance to be heard or communicate to others.

7. Begin interaction with activities that require little or no talking, and gradually add words.

8. Be genuine in your questions. Ask questions baby can answer. Do not give choices if any of the choices is not OK.

9. Follow the child's lead in the interaction by joining the baby's focus; then expand the play adding new ideas and meanings.

10. Show warmth and positive regard for the baby. Value baby's comments.

♣ FINGER PLAYS ♣

The Eensy, Weensy Spider

The eensy, weensy spider
crawled up the water spout.

Place forefinger on thumb of other
hand. Twirl around until opposite
thumb and forefinger meet - continue
in time, to "spout."

Down came the rain and washed
the spider out.

Raise arms and indicate falling rain
with fingers. Bring arms down with
outward motion.

Out came the sun and dried up all
the rain.

Raise arms in a circle over head to
make sun.

And the eensy, weensy spider
crawled up the spout again.

Repeat the forefinger on thumb
routine.

Here Is the Beehive

Here is the beehive.
Where are the bees?
Hidden away where nobody sees.
Watch and you'll see them.
Come out of the hive,
Bees - 1, 2 ,3, 4, 5
Fly away bees - Buzzz-z-z-z-z

Closed fists, palms inward.
Turn the fists about.

Show fingers beginning with thumb.
Flick fingers on flying hands.

Open, Shut Them

Open, shut them
Give a little clap
Open, shut them
Open, shut them
Lay them in your lap.
Creep them, creep them,
creep them, creep them.
Right up to your chin.
Open up your little mouth
But do not let them in!

Hold hands out in front.

Finger Plays, cont.

The Finger Band
(to tune of <u>Here We Go Round the Mulberry Bush</u>)

The finger band is coming to town, coming to town, coming to town.
The finger band is coming to town, so early in the morning.

Hands behind back and slowly bring them out in front.

This is the way they wear their caps, etc. ...

Hands pointed over head.

This is the way they play their <u>drums</u>, etc. ...

<u>Any instrument</u> may be illustrated.

The finger band is going away, going away, going away. The finger band is going away, so early in the morning.

Make soft voices.

The finger band has gone away, gone away, gone away.
The finger band has gone away, so early in the morning.

Very soft voices.

This Is My Right Hand
(follow hand directions explained in the verse)

This is my right hand,
I'll hold it up high.
This is my left hand,
I'll touch the sky.
Right hand, left hand.
Roll them around.
Left hand, right, hand,
... pound, pound, pound.

Little Jack Horner

Little Jack Horner
sat in a corner.   Place fist on lap.
Eating his Christmas pie;   Eating motions.
he put in his thumb
and pulled out a plum.   Stick thumb in.
And said, "What a   Pull out plum.
good boy am I!"
                            Pat self on head!

Two Little Feet
to go tap, tap, tap

Two little feet to go
tap, tap, tap
Two little hands to go
clap, clap, clap
A quick little leap
up from the chair.
Two little arms
reach high in the air.

Two little feet to go
jump, jump, jump
Two little hands to go
thump, thump, thump
One little body turns
round and round.
One little child
quietly sits down.

A+ Ideas for Reading to Your Baby

Read aloud together: Even an infant gains from hearing your voice. Lie on the bed quietly with your baby and read aloud. In the early months it does not need to be a children's book; it could be a computer manual. Your voice and your emotion do matter.

Zip through lots of books together: With baby or toddler on your lap, cruise the mail, magazines, newspaper, and books. Turn pages fast, point to what interests you (remember you are the model), and point to what might interest your baby.

Choose baby books with simple, familiar images: For first readers (8-14 mos.) choose cloth or cardboard books with large, simple pictures of items babies might see around them. Babies really like to see other babies, animals, and items they use or play with.

Animate the pictures in baby books: Do not read the words in the book, instead, make noises for animals, squeals for babies, play act useful items, like a toothbrush ("Brush, brush, brush"). If baby tries to copy your noises, encourage this. Soon you may have babies that read to themselves with noises or actions for what they see.

Keep books in the toy box: Have children's books around. Baby books are easy to get through the library and in drug stores and grocery stores. You can also make books which babies like by drawing or pasting pictures on cardboard. Toddlers like to help you make these books. Keep a book in baby's bed, a book near the car seat.

Use words babies know and can say: Use the words toddlers can say. Identify people in books, using names of people toddlers know. (This is like Mommy, this is like Daddy, this is like you!)

Wait for baby to read with you: As you identify pictures, pause for a bit and see if baby will try to say the word too. If baby wants to join in and tell you more about the pictures, wait and let baby add some ideas. Don't worry about the story line.

It is OK. to jump around in the book: Often babies want to jump to the end, or see a picture they love. It is good to let babies jump ahead to see what they like, jump back to see more of the story. You will be opening the door to new interests for these babies.

Read the same book over: This may seem boring for parents, but it is an attachment base for baby. Having the familiar pictures and story they know is a form of balance and equilibrium for baby. Some books become part of a routine, such as a bedtime story, or a story that Gramma always reads. Reading is play that leads to love.

Communication Review

1. Why is good communication important for you and your baby?

2. What are the two forms of communication?

3. Give four examples of nonverbal communication.

4. Diagram the steps in the process of the communication model?

5. What are the barriers to good communication?

6. What kinds of interferences block communication?

7. Why are finger plays important to your child's development?

—— Communicating
Word Search ——

**Thirteen special terms play a part in good communicating.
You'll find them hidden in the word search below.**

C - Copy
O - Oral
M - Message
M - Model
U - Understand
N - Nonverbal
I - Imitate
C - Conversation
A - Answer
T - Turn Taking
I - Information
N - Nodding
G - Giggle

```
M N R S T U L G E A C D P O Q N R M O D X
Q Z S P L C J N M N T C G I L X Y A O W C
P A R C L I O J R U C N V C O P Y N R Y B
Y C U D R N A N E N G R M L R O S S A E V
I E R P O B S E V D Q H P K U Y N W L U F
N J N E L T P O M E S S A G E V K E T A Z
F H N A Z D C I L R R I J N M X D R P G T
O O T N A K J A H S D S E L A O W I J W B
R R Z R V O B J C T F G A N M U H C O S L
M N X U B R T G F A K T J T H K I Q M V R
A P P O E A S E I N M U J L I M I T A T E
T T Y V O L J H M D L R V S P O T R L U T
I S N V Z R N D Q Y P N O D D I N G N Q R
O O R R G I G G L E R T E W O Z S H P J K
N U L N W J C T Z S X A U L Y T I X W O F
J E I M V B G X R V A K N I O X A G N A Y
R H K Z W Y U A W B Q I P D Z X V F B E E
T O F Y V X Q F I R P N J N H U B M C M G
Z X J Q Z A T C M S K G O K I C L D D H L
```

KEY for
Communicating Word Search

**Thirteen special terms play a part in good communicating.
You'll find them hidden in the word search below.**

Answer Key to Communicating Word Search

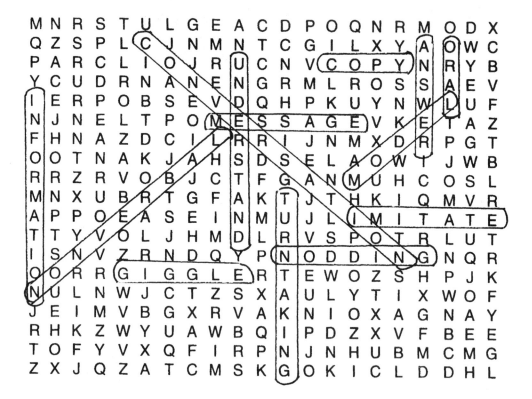

Playing Is Problem Solving

Playing Is Problem Solving

1. <u>Babies learn to solve problems through play</u>. They experiment with different ways to play with the same toy and learn something from each trial. Blocks can be chewed on, banged together, banged on the floor, put inside something, handed back and forth, or stacked in different ways. With blocks, toddlers can learn to copy your building or to create their own. They can pretend to build a train and go somewhere or build a house and live there. They are learning about options, what might be possible. They are problem solving.

When we solve a problem we feel competent. We feel internally pleased and strong. By gathering facts, watching others, and trying solutions, we solve our problems. This gives us a feeling of independence. Babies constantly strive to "get it right," to feel independent. Solving problems is one of the greatest feelings of mastery a person has. "I am in control; I am in charge of my life."

2. <u>Parents are the guides for their babies' problem solving</u>. They set the stage (define problem, set goal), provide the toys (tools and resources), suggest options (provide information and alternatives), stabilize trials (support systems), answer questions (identify facts and consequences), point out new directions (expand goals). They facilitate, support, and coach the learning process (they divide problems into small steps and praise strengths in baby). They share pride with their babies when a goal is gained. They <u>do not</u> do the task, or solve the problem for the baby.

3. <u>Parents make problem solving fun</u>. Parents ... who help babies have fun solving problems, share their curiosity, let them try new things and meet new people ... are expanding their minds and preparing them for independence. Problems such as "picking up" clothes or cleaning a spill can become a game when parents join in. This is how we learn to put tough challenges behind us ... by making them fun as well as challenging. When parents do this, they are raising babies who will continue to enjoy exploring, learning, and working on a task throughout life.

4. <u>Sharing the frustrations of problem solving is another important dimension of parenting</u>. It is easy to share interest, fun and pride with babies. It is harder to acknowledge the frustration, anger and sadness that can come with failure. Being aware of the fears which babies have because they are small, unsure or have failed in the past is an important parenting skill. When parents show understanding of their babies' frustrations or fears, when they label the feeling, "I know you must be angry," and when they can talk about it, they will help their babies grow emotionally.

5. <u>There is a readiness factor in problem solving</u>. When tasks are too hard or too new, babies withdraw and quickly refuse to try learning. When expectations for babies are true to each baby's developmental level, parents find success. If babies are not developmentally ready to solve a new task, they will not even try. Parents should model a new task several times, having fun doing it. Then, let babies explore the task on their own terms. Don't expect them to try to copy at first. Don't scold or fuss if they refuse a new toy, or make a mistake. Acknowledge the baby's feelings and try again at another time.

6. <u>Pretending is problem solving</u>. When toddlers pretend, they are problem solving about situations and relationships. Through pretend, they will try out different emotions. They imitate the actions they have seen modeled around them. They rehearse the rules they have learned. They review the fear of a moment on TV, trying to understand how it fits into their life. Pretending is mental problem solving.

Pretend play can also be a teaching tool. Parents can initiate a pretend situation to teach health habits, safety rules, and problem solving skills. In this way, they can define consequences and set patterns of behavior for the future.

7. <u>Problem solving teaches independence and mastery</u>. Independence is a lifelong need. Parents, who help their children gain independence, have happier children who are closer and more attached to them as well. This is an odd phenomena: when babies feel safe and "at one" with their parents, they move away and explore. They become more independent, able to stand alone. When parents provide emotional stability, their toddlers will become problem solvers and take on the challenges in life. However, they will continue to seek the closeness of their parents.

- How do babies learn to problem solve through play?
- How can parents help babies problem solve without doing the task?
- What should parents do if babies get frustrated or angry?
- Why does pretend play help problem solving?

Playing Is Problem Solving

Outcomes:

1. Parents will recognize how play teaches problem solving skills.
2. Parents will be able to analyze their babies' developmental readiness for problem solving tasks.
3. Parents will gain skill in managing their babies' problem solving play so that it is successful.
4. Parents will use pretend play as an effective way to teach babies problem solving.

Content and Concepts	Instructional Strategies for Parent Groups
INTRODUCTION: ❖Problem solving can be fun. •It challenges us. •It energizes us. •It gives us feelings of competence and independence.	Hang from the ceiling or scatter on the floor, a variety of different sized boxes. ◆Transparency "Box Problems" Discuss: 1. Why are the boxes here?" 2. How will you choose and negotiate the box you want? Using overhead ◆"Building Blocks for Problem Solving," discuss each block. Handout ◆"Solving My Problems." Parents use this to decide how to decorate this box. Display Instructor's Building Block #10 (see pg. 203)
KEY CONCEPTS: ❖For babies, problem solving is developmental. •Maturation allows a baby to remember solutions or consequences and think ahead to goals. •There is a readiness factor to problem solving. •Problem solving is successful when expectations are developmentally appropriate.	◆ Review handout: "Problem Solving Is Developmental." Illustrate by using Info. Sheet ◆"Object Permanence." Discuss how the ability to remember consequences or set goals evolves slowly over three years. Babies need parents as resources and mentors. Show video: Discoveries of Infancy: Cognitive Development and Learning.
	◆Using "Box Problems 3" answer "how can you and your baby play with your box?" Parents plan an age-appropriate game to play with baby using their box. This activity can be used during the Interactive Session.

❖Play is a way babies learn to solve problems.
 •Babies develop problem solving skills
  -by experimenting
  -by watching others
  -by practicing and expanding knowledge
	What kinds of problems are babies solving during play? (putting ball in box, picking up an object, etc.) How do they learn to solve these problems?
	
	◆Worksheet: "Baby Problems."

Instructional Strategies for Home Visitors

Terms to Understand

Ask parent how he or she solved a problem recently (e.g. car broke down, lost your keys, didn't have ingredients for recipe you were cooking) What did they do? How did they feel while they were solving the problem? After they solved the problem?

◆Discuss each step in solving a problem using "Building Blocks for Problem Solving and ◆"Solving My Problems" worksheets.

◆Review handout: "Problem Solving Is Developmental." Discuss how the ability to remember consequences or set goals evolves slowly over three years. Babies need parents as a resource and mentor. Use Info. sheet ◆"Object Permanence" as an example.

Show video: <u>Discoveries of Infancy: Cognitive Development and Learning</u>. Discuss concepts with parent and video's message? Is it true for your baby?

◆ Have parent complete an age-appropriate problem solving activity.

  •0-5 mos.: use PIPE card "Finding Sounds"
  (#7, Play Is Stimulating the Senses").
  •5-10 mos.: Use PIPE card "Three Toys"
  (#10, Playing While Learning About Differences).
  •10 mos. and older: Place paper grocery bags around the room or house. Hide a favorite toy or food in each and encourage baby to explore/find them.

Check baby's PDP.

Discuss how baby solved the problem.

<u>Alternatives</u>
Two or more choices for a single decision; different way to get to the same goal

<u>Consequences</u>
Something caused by an action or decision; what will happen

<u>Frustration</u>
A state of insecurity or dissatisfaction, and sometimes anger

<u>Intrude</u>
To enter in without invitation or welcome

<u>Object Permanence</u>
A maturational step which allows babies to comprehend that an object which is out of sight still exists

Content and Concepts	Instructional Strategies for Parent Groups

•Problem solving expands babies' brain.
 	
•Problem solving builds feelings of mastery.
 	
❖Relationships teach problem solving.
  •By experimenting, babies learn to define alternatives.
  •By seeking help, babies learn from models.
  •They find safety and support for their skills
  •They learn to define consequences.
 	
❖Pretend play helps babies solve problems.
  •Babies learn about emotions through pretending.
  •They act out relationship problems they have seen.
  •They re-live fearful, angry or happy experiences.
  •Parents can help toddlers manage problems through pretend play.
	<u>Discuss</u>:
	What happens when parents allow baby to try to solve problems by experimenting and exploring? Are babies solving problems when they play alone?
	
	◆Using "Building Blocks for Problem Solving," <u>brainstorm</u> how relationships help with problem solving?
	  -How does feeling safe help babies solve problems?
	  -How do parents help babies define consequences?
	<u>Have parents demonstrate</u> (using a child's puzzle) how to model, teach and scaffold while allowing exploration and mastery.
	
	◆Read together, and discuss, "Pretending Is Problem Solving Play."
	Read <u>Where the Wild Things Are</u> to parents.
	<u>Discuss</u> why books can help babies solve problems. How does this book help babies understand their emotions?
	
	◆<u>Using puppets, parents role play</u> situations described on "Puppet Play."

<u>Demonstration:</u>
Demonstrate with three different aged babies how the scaffolding technique can be used to teach problem solving. Can use boxes, peg board, puzzle, etc.
(See pages 86-87 for Scaffolding Technique.)

Evaluation/Closure

❖<u>Review</u>: PDP specific to problem solving development. List four problem solving activities you believe your baby will achieve this year.

Discuss:
What happens when parents allow baby to try to solve problems by experimenting and exploring?
Are babies solving problems when they play alone?

◆Using "Building Blocks for Problem Solving," discuss how babies might learn each step. How do relationships help with problem solving?
-How does feeling safe help baby solve problems?
-How do parents help baby define consequences?
Have parents demonstrate (using a child's puzzle) how to model, teach and scaffold while allowing exploration and mastery.

◆Read together, and discuss, "Pretend Is Problem Solving Play."
Read Where the Wild Things Are to parents.
Discuss why books can help babies solve problems. How does this book help babies understand their emotions?

Using puppets, or stuffed animals, role play how parent might teach about safety. Ask parent to demonstrate a topic from ◆"Puppet Play."

Priorities
Rated in order; ranked best to worst. The things you want most; what should happen first

Problem
A challenge, a puzzle; difficult to decide or deal with. An unsettled question or vexation

Rehearse
To practice; to repeat over and over
To recount or tell again

Resources
A source of information, knowledge or support; a possibility of relief or resolution

Verbal
Relating to or consisting of words

MATERIALS, SUPPLIES, & RESOURCES:

- •A variety of different sized boxes
- •Assorted art supplies
- •Transparencies
- •Video camera
- •Puppets, or supplies to make puppets
- •Video — Discoveries of Infancy: Cognitive Development & Infancy
- •Where the Wild Things Are (book)
- •Puzzle
- •Pegboard (optional)

INTERACTIVE SESSION

Activity: Practice using Scaffolding Technique with an activity where baby has to problem solve. The goal of this activity is to assist baby in problem solving by providing appropriate support and resources.

Hints for Success

Monitor interactions closely for successful use of the skills learned.

Videotape session, if possible.

Set the Stage:

1. ◆Review "Scaffolding Technique" Topic 4, page 86.

2. This session can integrate the skills from previous sessions. Review ◆ "Blocks of Pride," "Teaching the Do's," "Sharing Positive Emotions," "The Teaching Loop," and the "Mastery Cycle."

3. Parents set the stage by preparing box, puzzle, peg board or other activity ahead.

Supervised Interaction in Home Visits or Parent Groups:

☆1. Parents choose an age-appropriate problem solving activity for baby and use scaffolding technique to help baby be successful. Can use peg board, puzzle, boxes, etc.
  2. See directions and procedures in the Introduction (page vii).

Closure:

Review "Building Blocks for Problem Solving." Discuss how parent and baby used these blocks. Did baby solve the problem? Did baby enjoy the activity? How did parent assist?

Expansion/Enrichment:

•Have parents discuss times when they have used "Solving My Problems" in relation to their own problems.

TOPIC ENHANCERS

TOPIC:
Playing Is Problem Solving

For a Parent Group

1. Add topic poster, worksheets and information pages to parent's Play Portfolio.

2. Post "Building Blocks for Problem Solving" on bulletin board.

3. Make puppets for pretend play activities.

4. Create a library of baby books which teach or help a baby to problem solve. (i.e. questioning books, alphabet books, find-it books, predictable books)

5. Post the question "What Is a Problem?" on bulletin board.

For Parents at Home

•Make a list of or journal about problems you have solved and how you solved them.

•Make a storybook which teaches baby about a problem that is age-appropriate.

•Make hand puppets for you and family members to play pretend with baby.

•Discuss how babies use behaviors which parents don't like, when problems are too hard or expectations too high. Using "DOOZYs" (see Appendix), discuss with your home visitor ways to manage such behaviors.

Box Problems

Problem 1
Why are the boxes here?

Problem 2
How do you decide which will be your box?

Problem 3
How could you and your baby play with the box?

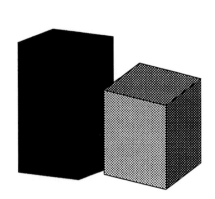

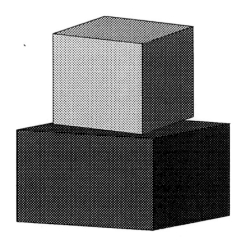

Building Blocks to Problem Solving

Identify for problem
- Whose problem is it?
- Why is it a problem?
- What is your goal?

Gather Information
- Communicate... share... learn.
- Gather resources, advisors, experts and books.
- Find mentors, models and support systems.

Define Alternatives
- Set several solutions.
- Define a plan for each solution.

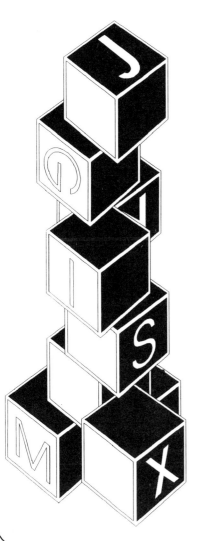

Define Consequences
- What will be the result of each solution in a week, a month, a year?
- Who else will this decision affect?

Identify Your Strengths and Skills
- What do I know?
- What am I good at?
- Do I have good helpers?

Divide Problem Into Small Steps
- What is the simplest thing I could change?
- What is the most important thing to change?

Take Action

Congratulate Yourself for Each Step Accomplished

Solving My Problems

This is my problem ...

These are my choices of what to do:	... And the consequences (good and bad):	
1.	a.	a.
2.	b.	b.
3.	c.	c.
4.	d.	d.

These are my helpers and resources:

1.

2.

3.

This is my best choice:

and my plan to do it is: **steps I need to make this happen.**

❖ Baby Problems ❖

	List Play Activities or Toys babies enjoy at each age	What problem will baby be solving with this activity or toy?
0-3 mos.		
3-6 mos.		
6-9 mos.		
9-12 mos.		
12-18 mos.		
18-24 mos.		
2-3 yrs.		

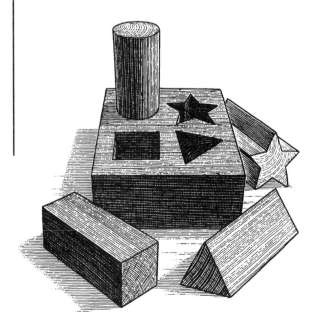

Object Permanence

Learning to problem solve is developmental. Most of a baby's brain matures after birth. It is good nutrition, consistent caregiving, and the sensory experiences which develop strong nerve connections for the growing brain. As this happens, babies become more able to remember and to plan ahead.

For instance, infants first learn that there is a relationship between their sensations, such as their feeling of touch and their mown movements. Very quickly they learn that they can pull away from a sensation or reach toward it. New connections are made in their brains. "I can reach and touch. My hand is connected to me. I am in control!" A new world of challenge appears. But ... if the ball rolls out of sight, the infant turns to something else. It is as if the ball vaporized.

In the last half of the first year, babies' brains mature to a new level. They can now remember the ball when they can't see it. They look for it and find it. They quickly learn that the ball still exists somewhere. This is called the Principle of Object Permanence.

Now the baby has a new level of problem solving ability. Peek-a-boo games become fun for baby. Babies can make choices and see differences in people and objects around them. They can define who they want to be with and what things they like.

Try hiding an object that your baby likes under your box. Be sure baby sees you hide it. Does baby try to discover it under the box? Has your baby developed Object Permanence?

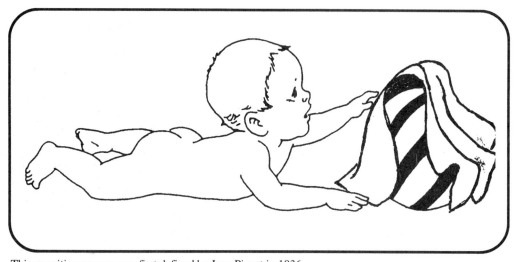

This cognitive process was first defined by Jean Piaget in 1936.

Problem Solving Is Developmental

0-3 mos.	"How does my body work? Who will take care of me? How will I survive? How do I find balance?"
3-6 mos.	"I control my body! My hands, my feet, my voice! What can I reach? What can I taste? What does my voice say? Who do I influence?"
6-9 mos.	"How do I get attention? How do I get what I want? How can I make interesting things happen? What are all these objects for?"
9-12 mos.	"I can crawl. I can move away, go anywhere. It is fun and scary. I might be all alone. Who do I copy, who is my guide? Who will help me? Who will show me? How do I keep my parents close?"
12-18 mos.	"I can walk now. I remember my parents. I remember my friends. I have favorite toys, foods, and things. I demand what I want. I have tantrums if I'm told no and then I feel alone. How do I get along? How do I "fit in" and belong?
18-24 mos.	" I can talk now, I can feed myself, put things together. My parents give me problems to solve, choices to make. They take me interesting places. They give me rules and instructions. I get confused and frustrated. Who will help me?
2-4 years	"I'm learning a lot. I go to other places, meet other kids, other caregivers. I remember what I have learned and how to solve problems the way my parents showed me. It works with new friends and in new places. I feel confident. I can keep learning and meeting the challenge each new day."

Based on the works of Piaget, this chart illustrates how problem solving evolves as baby develops.

Pretending Is Problem Solving

Pretend play is problem solving.

When toddlers are pretending, they are problem solving about relationships.
They try out different emotions and situations which they have watched.
They imitate the actions they have seen modeled around them.
They rehearse the rules they have learned.
They review the fear of a moment on TV.

Pretend is a way to see consequences.

By play acting several different endings to a situation, toddlers can begin
to see what might happen in the future.

Pretend is a way to understand others. By playing the role of another,
a toddler can feel the other person's experience. If a toddler pours juice
for her doll and the doll spills it, the toddler understands how a parent
might feel.

Pretend is a way to set priorities.

By pretending, toddlers can practice several different outcomes to the same play.
This allows them to think about which is the best.

Pretend is a way to copy adults.

By pretending, toddlers can act like the people they see and hear around them.
This is why one-year-olds like telephones and kitchen toys.

Pretend is a way to practice different emotions.

Pretend is a way for toddlers to try many emotions. It is a way to express anger
or sadness. It is a way to tell their feelings to another pretend person or
to their toys.

Fear is quieted or enhanced by pretend play. Using their toys re-enact fearful
times is a way to try to understand their fear. If parents have had a fight,
the toddler will often relive this with toys. Sometimes, toddlers need adults to help
 them find a happy ending to fearful pretend plays.

Often pretend play is a "private" affair for toddlers. They do not want adults to
join in. They may quit pretending or get angry if a parent intrudes.

Adults also pretend.
Most adults rehearse their actions or their feelings about an important
challenge in their minds or even in front of a mirror. ... This is healthy.

Pretend play can be a teaching tool.

Parents can teach important lessons with pretend play. They can invent a pretend situation to teach health habits, safety rules, and problem solving skills. In this way, they can define consequences and set patterns of behavior for the future. It is a way to teach toddlers to think ahead. It is a way to make problem solving more positive.

Pretend play can be a family way to share fun.

"Let's go swimming," says Dad. He makes a circle on the floor with a string and then jumps inside and pushes his arms in front of him as if swimming.

Baby squeals and jumps in also. Mom puts her toe in the pool and says, "Oh, that's cold!"

Baby jumps and says, "Come in, come in, I'll splash you!"

Puppet Play

Using puppets, or stuffed animals, a parent can use different voices and pretend a scene which the toddler may not yet have experienced.

"Look! Mr. Dog, here is a big street. Let's run across.

Oh, No! Miss Squirrel, we must be careful. Cars and trucks can hurt us. We must stop and look first."

Role play with puppets the following ideas or rules for toddlers. How does your pretend play teach a solution to a problem?

1. Sharp objects are dangerous.

2. Do not play with matches.

3. That's too hot for baby to touch.

4. Why do we share toys?

5. Going to the doctor

6. How to treat a pet

Playing Is Learning

Closure

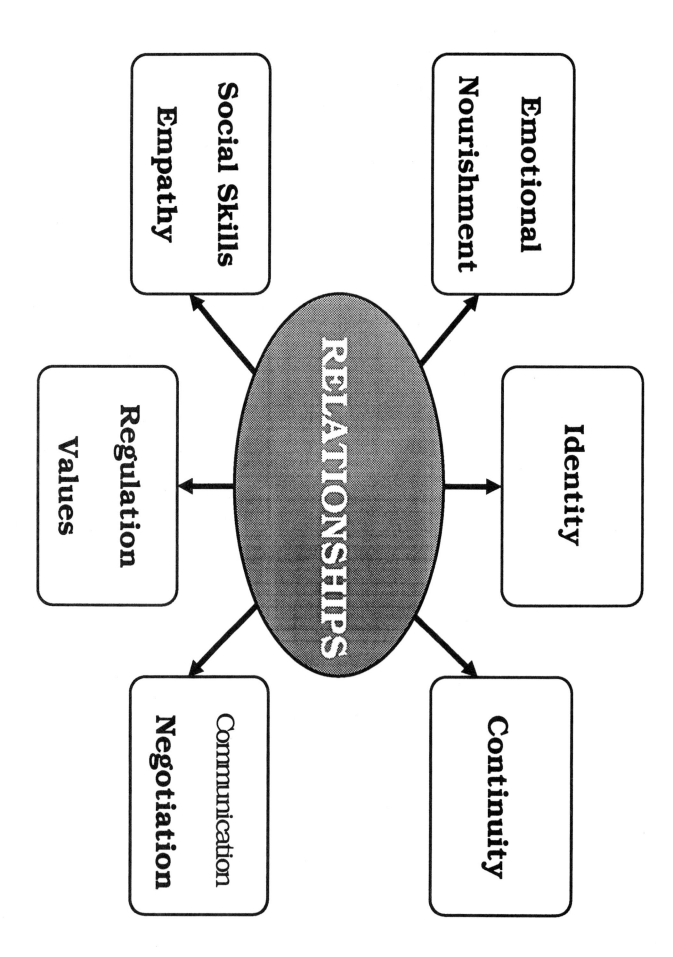

RELATIONSHIPS

Emotional Nourishment

Social Skills Empathy

Regulation Values

Communication Negotiation

Identity

Continuity

Emde/Butterfield

Relationships Are Key to Learning

1. <u>Babies are naturally motivated to learn</u>. There seems to be an inner voice which activates the newborn to look around, listen move and connect their brains to sensory input. The drive to explore, practice and master new things is powerful in the infant and toddler. This, of course, is how all species become adults and survive.

2. <u>Relationships are key to babies' continued learning</u>. It is through relationships that the motivation to learn is supported and enriched. It is through relationships that babies gain feelings of safety and acceptance which give them the confidence to continue learning.

3. <u>Babies are naturally motivated to find equilibrium</u>. Most healthy newborns self-regulate and set predictable patterns of eating, being alert or drowsy, and sleeping. This predictable patterns gives them the physiologic organization needed to learn and to survive. As they join the more complex world of their parents, they will seek emotional nourishment and emotion regulation from others. Relationships provide stability.

4. <u>Babies are naturally motivated to connect with other humans</u>. The newborn turns to a human face, brightens to a human voice, quiets to a human touch. This connection with another human (usually a parent) is an emotional connection, a feeling of "shared space" and shared understanding. This emotional connection gives meaning to the sensory experiences babies are receiving. When the emotional connection is positive, it conveys confidence, value and creativity to babies. When it is consistently available, it gives babies a sense of continuity and a feeling of trust that the same pattern or procedure can be expected and remembered. This gives babies confidence in their learning.

5. <u>Babies are naturally motivated to belong</u>. Survival for all species is dependent on quickly learning about the dangers and the rules of behavior within their group. By six to nine months of age, most babies identify one or two special relationships which provide them with a model to copy. These relationships set babies' first limits and rules. They set patterns of collaboration and negotiation. They provide a model for social interaction. They establish the "do's and don'ts" of a family. They set the values of the group or culture. It is from these first relationships that babies establish enduring patterns of socialization.

6. <u>Play is a natural pathway for learning</u>. It is also a natural path for relationships to be strengthened. It is a way to share, to collaborate and to expand skills and knowledge. Playing is a way we share positive emotions. Play is a valuable teacher. So, "make time for fun, ... Get down and play with your child."

Closure: Relationships Are Key to Learning

Outcomes:

1. Parents will demonstrate their understanding of how they help their babies to learn.
2. Parents will identify the skills they have learned for expanding and supporting babies' learning.
3. Parents will analyze how Shared Positive Emotions and Calm, Controlled Emotions enhance babies' learning.

Content and Concepts	Instructional Strategies for Parent Groups
INTRODUCTION: ❖Playing Is Learning is about how relationships and play activities influence learning.	Using *Word Burst* game, have each student write on his or her own page as many words as possible in one minute about why playing is important to learning. Using these words, discuss how relationships influence learning.
•Playing and Sharing Positive Emotions (SPE) give babies balance and confidence for learning.	Handout and complete a blank outline of ◆"Positive Emotions Propel Learning" (see Topic 5, page 105). Discuss how play and SPE influence learning.
•Playing sets patterns which strengthen babies' learning.	Discuss how patterns, rhythms, and routines help organize babies for learning.
•Play with others sets rules and goals for collaboration and negotiation.	Parents are teaching the rules of the family and values of their group or culture. Complete the blank outline of ◆"The Super Cs" (KEY, Topic 6, page 135).
KEY CONCEPTS: ❖Babies are naturally motivated to •find equilibrium, a sense of balance; •explore, master, be independent' •connect emotionally in a safe, shared space; •belong to the group, know the rules, "fit in."	List on the black board and discuss: the internal motives that push babies, especially toddlers, to learn. (You can have parents name famous songs for each of these motivations, i.e. "I'll Do It My Way," Sinatra)
❖Understanding babies is important to helping them learn.	

❖Parents give stability to babies.

❖Parents help socialize babies.

❖The first relationship is the first teacher.
  •Parents provide the protection, the model, the guidance, and the emotional connection for babies' learning and babies' future.
  •Play is a natural way to make relationships strong and positive.

◆<u>Review</u> "What Babies Learn In the First Year. Use poster, ◆"Stability" (see Topic 4, page 81). Complete the blanks to discuss how parents give babies emotional balance and organize them for learning.

◆<u>Review</u> "What Babies Learn In the Second Year. Use poster, ◆"Socialization" (see Topic 4, page 83). Complete the blanks to discuss how parents help babies learn to "fit in" and belong. They model and teach emotional control, rules and limits, language and social skills.

◆<u>Complete Worksheet</u> "What skills have you learned?"

Expansion and Enrichment

•Write a paragraph about your baby. Tell where you have stabilized your baby and how you have, or will, socialize your baby.

•Using photos of your baby, make a collage of development, showing changes and fun times you have shared together.

•Make a grab basket of ideas for a "Games" file. Parents write interactive games which they have enjoyed with their babies and put them on 3" x 5 cards in a classroom basket. Each parent draws out one card in order to begin a "Games" card file for him/herself and his/her baby.

•Start an SPE Group: Parents find others they would like to meet with regularly in the summer or at other times for a babies' play group. Parents set a time for the first "SPE Group" meeting.

Positive Emotions Propel Learning

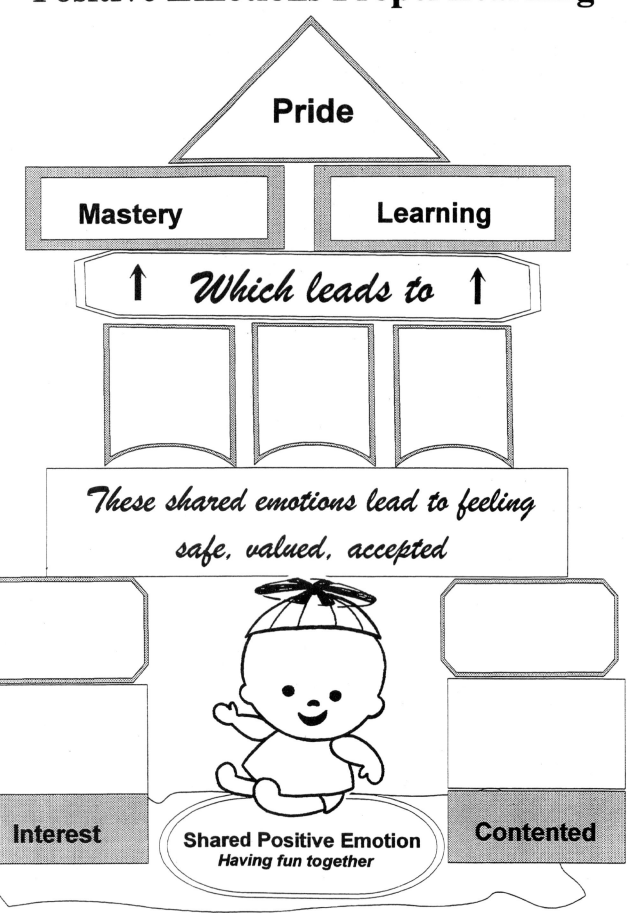

Pride

Mastery

Learning

↑ *Which leads to* ↑

These shared emotions lead to feeling safe, valued, accepted

Interest

Shared Positive Emotion
Having fun together

Contented

The Super C's
Clear, Calm Controlled Negative Emotions

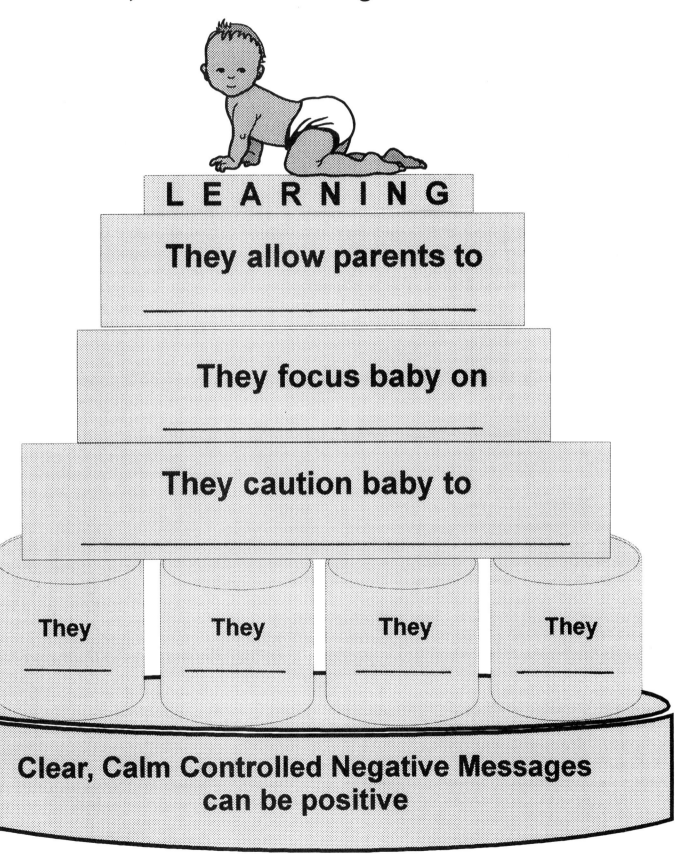

L E A R N I N G

They allow parents to
_____

They focus baby on
_____

They caution baby to
_____

They   They   They   They
_____   _____   _____   _____

**Clear, Calm Controlled Negative Messages
can be positive**

Stability

❖ **The first relationship is the Foundation for Learning.**

❖ **Parents provide the feelings of stability which allow learning to occur.**

These feelings are:

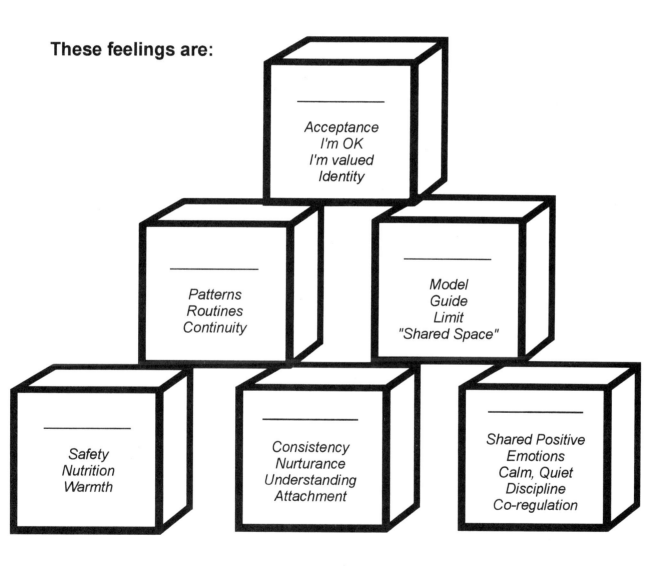

*Acceptance
I'm OK
I'm valued
Identity*

*Patterns
Routines
Continuity*

*Model
Guide
Limit
"Shared Space"*

*Safety
Nutrition
Warmth*

*Consistency
Nurturance
Understanding
Attachment*

*Shared Positive
Emotions
Calm, Quiet
Discipline
Co-regulation*

— ·· — Socialization — ·· —

❖ **The first relationship sets the pattern for all others.**

❖ **By modeling and teaching, parents show baby how to belong and learn from others.**

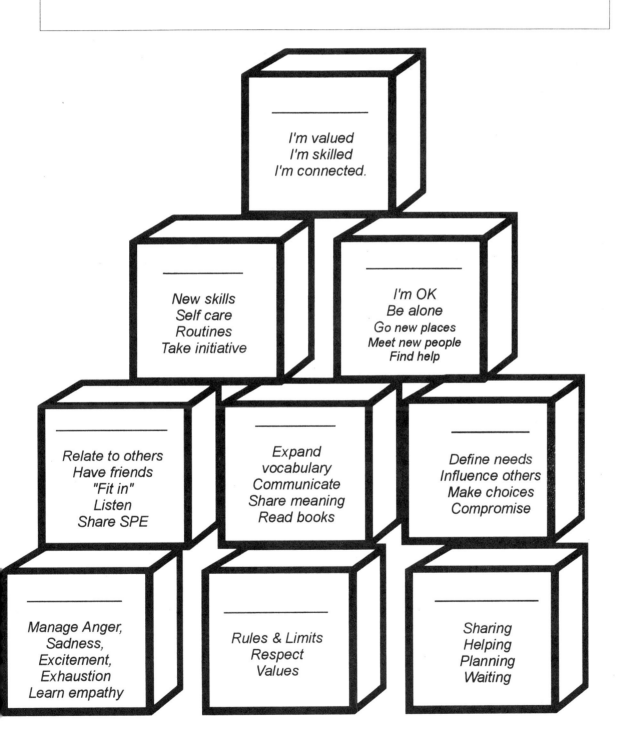

I'm valued
I'm skilled
I'm connected.

New skills
Self care
Routines
Take initiative

I'm OK
Be alone
Go new places
Meet new people
Find help

Relate to others
Have friends
"Fit in"
Listen
Share SPE

Expand
vocabulary
Communicate
Share meaning
Read books

Define needs
Influence others
Make choices
Compromise

Manage Anger,
Sadness,
Excitement,
Exhaustion
Learn empathy

Rules & Limits
Respect
Values

Sharing
Helping
Planning
Waiting

Parenting Skills I Have Learned

Write two things you have learned about each topic listed below.

What have you learned about:

1. How to Communicate with your baby?

     a.

     b.

2. How to start Turn-Taking with your baby?

     a.

     b.

3. When to find and use Teachable Moments?

     a.

     b.

4. How to help baby Solve Problems?

     a.

     b.

5. How to Regulate and Stabilize a fussy baby?

     a.

     b.

6. How to Regulate and Re-direct an angry baby?

     a.

     b.

7. Why are Schedules and Patterns important?

     a.

     b.

8. Why are Parents important in the first two years?

     a.

     b.

9. Who will help you when you are not feeling up to the job?

     a.

     b.

Appendix

Date: Name _____

Topic _____

Checking What I Learned

1. I learned ...

2. I realized ...

3. I noticed ...

4. I discovered ...

5. I was surprised ...

6. I was pleased ...

7. I was displeased ...

8. I re-learned ...

Topic _____   **BABY'S <u>FACE CHECK</u>**

Parent _____

I think _____ reaction to today's activities was ...
        (Child's name)

because:

· ·

Topic _____   **<u>PARENT'S FACE CHECK</u>**

Parent _____

My reaction to today's activities was ...

because:

Topic Activity Sheet

| Unit & Topic: | DATE: |
| Child's Name | Age |

Activities Selected	Parent's Comments & Evaluation	Supervisor's Comments

Name _____ GRADE _____

"Doozys"

What Do Babies Do to Un-do Parents?

For Home Visitors: The subject of discipline is a major concern to many home visitors. As home visitors, you have the opportunity to work individually with parents and to address the authoritarian styles which are detrimental to the equilibrium and socialization of the infant and toddler. Every Topic in this volume defines skills for regulating behavior and for avoiding behavioral difficulties. For those who want to invest your parent/client(s) in a more direct discussion of discipline, each Topic also includes a worksheet to open the discussion. These pages called ◆"DOOZYS: What *do* babies *do* to un-*do* Parents?" They are suggested for use in the "Topic Enhancers for Parents at Home" sections of each Topic.

Answer Key to the "DOOZYs" pages, which follow:

Topic 1:
3, 1, 6, 5, 4, 2

Topic 2:
6, 5, 4, 2, 1, 3

Topic 3:
4, 6, 2, 5, 1, 3

Topic 4:
2, 3, 1, 6, 4, 5

Topic 5:
This entire topic is about "*do's.*"

Topic 6:
3, 2, 1, 6, 5, 4

Topic 7:
4, 5, 2, 6, 1, 3

Topic 8:
3, 6, 2, 5, 1, 4

Topic 9:
3, 5, 1, 4, 6, 2

Topic 10:
4, 6, 2, 5, 1, 3

"Doozys"

What **Do** Babies **Do** to Un-**do** Parents?

Curiosity and Mastery

Babies' natural inclination to explore and master new things leads them to do things their parents may not like. Discuss together ways to manage these and other behaviors which are bothersome.

What do babies do?	What should parents do?
_____ My baby makes ugly noises: gargling, screeching, spitting.	1. Child proof the house for a short time and let baby explore.
_____ My baby goes from one thing to another and never focuses on a task or toy.	2. So what's a mess? It's a learning experience. Give him a spoon and let him "go for it"!
_____ My baby wants to go through my purse or the diaper bag.	3. Baby wants to see your reaction. Ignore the bad; copy the good.
_____ My baby drops everything off his high chair. I pick it up and down it goes again!	4. Give baby some cupboards to explore safely. Keep others off limits. Put a lock on all unsafe places. Exploration is learning!
_____ My baby is opening cupboards and drawers and getting into dangerous stuff.	5. Baby is learning about gravity. Either join the game or ignore it.
_____ My baby wants to feed himself, but makes too much mess.	6. Clear the deck. Open your purse. Check for unsafe items. Let baby explore (keys, glasses case, etc.).

When my baby does _____,   I do _____.

"Doozys"

What Do Babies Do to Un-do Parents?

Individual Differences
Babies' changing abilities lead them to do things their parents may not like.
Discuss together ways to manage these and other behaviors which are bothersome.

What do babies do?	What should parents do?
_____ My baby pulls on my hair, glasses, and earrings.	1. Baby will need some place to practice which is trouble free. Can you confine baby in a safe play space?
_____ My baby cries and fusses whenever I leave.	2. Stay calm. Take a big breath. Ask "why?" Do you need to ignore or can you fix? Isolate tantrums. Use five minute rule to return to comfort Baby.
_____ My baby doesn't like the food I fix.	
_____ My baby gets so mad, he will scream for 10 minutes.	3. Wanting to walk is an amazing drive. Babies will do nothing else until they master the skill. You are stuck supporting the baby through this stage.
_____ My baby is crawling and getting stuck behind furniture. He is crying for me all the time.	4. New things are hard for some babies. Try taking a bite of new food with a bite of familiar food. Eat some yourself. Don't expect too much the first time. Let baby eat new things off of your plate.
_____ My baby won't sit and play. She just wants to walk with me holding her hand every minute of the day.	
	5. This is normal. Baby is saying he loves you. Tell baby you will be back. Give him a teddy. Tell baby he is safe. Leave promptly once you have said good-bye.
	6. Gently hold baby's hands, make sad noises, "That hurts me. Owwie!" Divert. If it persists, put baby down. This is a stage. It will go away.

When my baby does _____, 　　　　I do _____.

"DOOZYs"

What Do Babies Do to Un-do Parents?

Baby's First Teacher

When babies want attention or dislike caretaking routines, teaching them something interesting is a good behavior regulator. Discuss together ways to manage these and other behaviors which are bothersome.

What do babies do?	What should parents do?
_____ My baby fusses about putting on socks and shoes.	1. Turn baby around. Show baby how to slide on tummy one step at a time. Stay close so baby feels safe to learn.
_____ My baby bothers me when I'm busy.	2. Have a drawer with adult things a baby can play with. Show baby "his or her drawer." Say, "No, these are Mama's. Here are yours."
_____ My baby wants to use my things and do what I am doing.	3. Babies like routines. They become very attached to what they know is theirs. Buy baby a second special cup so he can feel ownership.
_____ My baby pulls on my leg when I'm cooking.	4. Sing "this little piggy" and play with baby's toes. Puts socks on and gently tickle baby's knees. Put shoes on.
_____ My baby wobbles on the top step, reaching for me.	5. Baby wants your attention. Pick baby up and show baby what you are doing. Let baby help or give baby a task which is like yours.
_____ My baby wants the same cup and spoon for every meal.	6. Put baby in a high chair near you. Give baby a dish of Cheerios and/or something to do.

When my baby does _____,   I do _____.

"*Doozy*s"

What **Do** Babies **Do** to Un-**do** Parents?

What Are Babies Really Learning?
When babies are learning how to behave and to manage their emotions, they do things their parents may not like. Discuss together ways to manage these and other behaviors which are bothersome.

What do babies do?	What should parents do?
____ My toddler still sucks her thumb all the time.	1. Car seat use is a law we must follow. You can make it more fun with new toys every few days. Talk and sing so baby doesn't feel lonely. Baby may have to "cry his frustration out." Be clear and firm; the rule stands.
____ My toddler screams and has tantrums for no reason.	2. Thumb sucking is about emotional regulation. She is feeling unsure. Her thumb gives her stability. Be sure she gets lots of assurance from you.
____ My baby hates to sit in the car seat. He likes to sit on my lap.	3. Tantrums show frustration. They are normal for a toddler. Think about what happened before the tantrum. Has baby had much free choice lately? Has your style been controlling?
____ My baby hides her head whenever we meet new people.	4. It is hard to share. Give your baby another attractive toy or take your baby somewhere else. Then give your baby the original toy back when it is free.
____ My baby takes toys away from others ... screams when I give them back.	5. Tell baby dogs aren't toys. When dogs are mad they bite the other dog's face. That is why most dogs fear hugs. Dogs like pats. "We <u>do</u> pat. We don't hug."
____ My toddler hugs every dog he sees.	6. Baby is unsure. She is watching you to see how you act. Your behavior will guide her and give her confidence. Soon she will be ready to be social.

When my baby does _____,   I do _____

"Doozys"

What Do Babies Do to Un-do Parents?

Roadblocks to Learning

Toddlers' natural initiative and unschooled emotions cause them to challenge their parents'
rules and limits. Discuss together ways to manage these and other behaviors which are bothersome.

What do babies do?	What should parents do?
_____ My toddler screams and has fits when I take something away.	1. Baby is imitating you, not opposing you. Say, "That's right; that's a no." Then take action. Gently remove baby from the problem.
_____ My baby grabs for my food instead of her own.	2. Babies want desperately to grow up. If you can, give baby some of your food on her dish. Also, feed baby in her own chair, not in your lap.
_____ My baby says "NO, NO," every time I say NO."	3. It makes most of us mad to have things taken from us. Say," I know you're angry, but this will hurt you. Do you want this instead? If baby still screams, walk away.
_____ My baby runs away from me when he has been bad.	4. Take action. This shouldn't become a game. Gently remove the toy or the baby. Be clear and calm, but sure. Time out (1-5 min.) is effective by 12 months of age.
_____ My baby doesn't listen when I say "stop it."	5. Listening is hard for all of us. Babies' memories are also short. Be sure you have your baby's attention, pick baby up, or gently hold baby's face toward you. Use the three warnings rule. Then take action to change the situation.
_____ When I say "no" my baby laughs and goes right ahead and does it.	6. Running away from a scolding is ok. This means baby already knows he was wrong. The point is to stop the bad behavior. Baby doesn't really need a scolding. Just ignore him; don't chase.

When my baby does _____,   I do _____

"Doozys"

What **Do** Babies **Do** to Un-**do** Parents?

Stimulation of the Senses

Babies enjoy finding new sensory experiences. This can lead them to do things which can annoy their parents. Discuss together ways to manage these and other behaviors which are bothersome.

What do babies do?	What should parents do?
_____ When we go to the Mall, my baby lasts about half an hour and then starts fussing.	1. Say, "No, dirty water." Shut the lid. Take baby to play in some clean water in sink or pan. Find water toys.
_____ My baby dumps her food on the table and messes in it.	2. Changing sound by touching a button is a powerful sensory experience. Put TV or the remote up high.
_____ My baby turns all the knobs on the TV. He changes channels and volume.	3. The stimulations of the day can build nervous tensions. Try a back rub, infant massage, or quiet room to relax baby.
_____ My baby puts everything in her mouth.	4. Is baby too hot? Is baby hungry? A snack can often change fussing to smiles.
_____ My baby plays in the toilet.	5. Food play is fun! This is like finger painting. You spoon food into her mouth and let her have fun feeling the food. This stage will pass.
_____ By the end of the day, my baby is so fussy it drives me crazy.	6. This is a stage. The mouth provides early sensory learning. Give baby teething rings or biscuits. Clear the house of unsafe objects and watch baby closely.

When my baby does _____,   I do _____.

"Doozys"

What **Do** Babies **Do** to Un-**do** Parents?

Imitation and Reciprocal Turn-Taking

The natural urge to imitate can lead babies toward behaviors that are dangerous or annoying.
Discuss together ways to manage these and other behaviors which are bothersome.

What do babies do?	What should parents do?
_____ My baby gets into my jewelry. She wants to wear my beads and bracelets.	1. Babies become "one" with their models. They believe they can become Batman, have magic, or do adult things. Parents need to be vigilant.
_____ My baby wants to feed me when he is on my lap at the table.	2. Marking and drawing is an exciting mastery skill. Keep pencils and colors out of reach during this early imitation phase. Plan special times to color when you can provide super-vision.
_____ My baby colors on the walls and marks with pencil on everything.	
_____ My baby hits and kicks at the dog and other kids.	3. Your baby wears your beads to be like you. Find some beads baby can wear safely.
_____ My baby begs for his Batman shirt and then tries to jump off the bed or counter!	4. Boys love to pretend and model their mothers <u>and</u> fathers. Face painting is fun for all of us.
_____ My baby gets my makeup from my purse and puts it all over his face. Is he a real boy?	5. What has baby seen on TV or seen others do? Put a stop to the kicking and define what or who is the model. Give baby another way to feel powerful.
	6. Feeding you is imitation and turn-taking. You can play the game and take a bite, or set limits and say "no, you feed yourself."

When my baby does _____ ,   I do _____.

"Doozys"

What Do Babies Do to Un-do Parents?

Communicating Is Not Always Easy

It is hard to connect with a baby. Often the baby doesn't get the message or doesn't seem to want to learn. Discuss together ways to manage these and other behaviors which are bothersome.

What do babies do?	What should parents do?
_____ My baby tears the pages when I try to read to her.	1. Don't insist. Turn away and ignore her. Do something else. She is saying "no" to test her power. Return soon to do the task with fun in your voice.
_____ My baby bangs on the toys and squeals, He won't play like I show him.	2. Set clear limits. Strike a contract with Baby. "Only two books." Let Baby help choose the books; then you both stick to the bargain.
_____ My baby says "no" when I tell her to do something and then screams when I insist.	3. Gently hold baby's hand and say, "No, no, don't tear. Look, Zoom! Plane."
_____ My baby wants the same toy over and over. How can we learn new things together	4. The toy is like a "safe base." It gives baby balance. Baby will be learning, because baby will try something new, even with the old toy.
_____ Sarah talks when I'm trying to tell her what I want. She doesn't listen.	5. Baby may be too young for these toys. Join baby, bang on the toy also. Then find a pounding toy or blocks to bang. You will connect at baby's level.
_____ Max wants to read every book before bed. He doesn't hear me say it's bed time.	6. She talks because she wants to communicate too. Spend some time listening to her. Then say, "Now it's my turn, Sarah. Listen."

When my baby does _____,   I do _____

I do _____.

"Doozys"

What Do Babies Do to Un-do Parents?

Problem Solving

Sometimes being a parent seems full of problems.
Discuss together ways to manage these and other behaviors which are bothersome.

What do babies do?	What should parents do?
_____ My one-year-old has stopped eating. She was doing well on solids; now she just picks at food.	1. It is time for a big bed. Put a mattress with bedding on the floor as baby's bed. Put a baby gate on the door for safety and make baby's room safe to prowl.
_____ My baby has started waking up at night. Does he need a snack or a bottle?	2. Spend more playful, fun time with baby. Be sure <u>you</u> get baby up and put baby to bed.
_____ My baby likes Grandma better than me.	3. Make time out shorter and somewhere where baby can see you, even in a big chair or a corner. Forgive baby quickly.
_____ My baby has terrible tantrums. We can't seem to quiet her.	4. Eating less is common for new walkers. They don't have time to stop and eat. Don't worry. It will change.
_____ My baby climbs out of the crib.	5. Tantrums show frustration. Try giving your toddler more control, more choice. Also explain to her ahead of time what is going to happen and what her job will be.
_____ My baby won't stay in "time out."	6. Night waking is common around 12 months. Babies may be looking for security. Hold baby and calmly put baby down again.

When my baby does _____,   I do _____.

Ideas for Toys
To Promote Learning

Texture Sticks

Materials: Round, flat ended clothes pins or tongue depressors; material scraps, permanent markers

Pick fabrics that have interesting textures. Glue pieces of these fabrics around the base of the clothes pins or depressors. Draw faces on the uncovered part of the wood.

Texture Gloves

Materials: An old glove, material scraps, needle and thread or a glue gun
Pick fabrics that have interesting textures. Cut a piece of textured fabric. Sew or glue to fingers and palm of the glove.

Spoon Friends

Materials: 7" wooden spoon; 4" piece of ribbon; permanent ink markers; glue gun
Draw a happy face on front of the spoon and a sad face on the back.
Tie ribbon around the handle for a bow and glue bow securely.

Spicy Socks

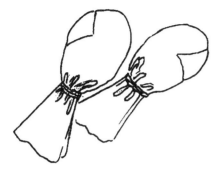

Materials: Small socks, cotton, smelly spices, rubber bands
Sprinkle spices onto cotton balls. Stuff them into the toes of the socks. Wrap a rubber band around each sock to hold in the cotton ball.

Roly Poly Book

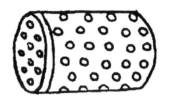

Materials: Oatmeal container with lid; magazines with pictures; scissors; clear contact paper.
Select pictures familiar to baby from magazine. Cut them out and glue them on round container. Let glue dry and cover with clear contact paper.

Picture Book

Materials: Construction paper; yarn; hole punch; simple pictures from coloring books; crayons; markers; glue.
Fold three sheets of construction paper in half and crease. Punch two holes. Thread and tie them with yarn. In coloring books find and color pictures of things baby is familiar with (teddy bears, puppies, etc.). Glue one picture on each page. [Optional to cover with clear contact paper.]

Noisy Boxes

Materials: Assorted small boxes; small pasta noodles; colorful contact paper; glue gun
Fill small boxes one quarter full of pasta noodles. Glue the lids shut. Cover with colorful contact paper.

Touch Books

Materials: Three 8" x 12" pieces of cotton fabric with edges cut with pinking shears; assorted pieces of textured fabrics; glue gun or sewing supplies.

Place each piece of 8" x 12" fabric on top of each other and sew a seam down the middle (or glue them together). Cut textured fabric into interesting shapes (ABCs, Baby's name; shapes of animals or toys; squares, triangles, circles, etc.) Glue onto cloth pages.

Poke Box

Materials: Egg carton or plastic ice cube tray; assorted textured materials (cotton balls, sandpaper, velvet, etc.); glue.
Cut the lid off the egg carton or use clean, dry ice cube tray.
Cut textured materials to fit into each section of the box or tray. Glue each piece securely into the section.

Scented Play Dough

Materials: 2 and one-half cups flour
one-half cup salt
2 cups boiling water
1 Tbs. alum
3 Tbs. cooking oil
1 to 3 pkgs. unsweetened Kool-Aid (# of packages
will determine the intensity of the color and the scent)

Mix salt, flour, alum and Kool-Aid together. Add boiling water and stir quickly. Add oil and mix well. When cool enough, mix with hands. Store in air-tight container in refrigerator.

Other Playful Ideas
for Sharing and Learning

Play Dough Party

Parents can experience the senses at work. Using scented play dough and play dough tools, have parents make several batches of play dough in different scents and colors.

Have parents play with their babies and the play dough to stimulate all of the senses. Be aware of the different feelings which the colors, smells and sounds bring out in all of the individuals who are participating.

Pot Luck Picnic

Parents can experience outdoor sights and sounds while exploring different tastes and smells.

Make up a poster with different tastes on it and have the parents sign up ahead of time to bring foods which fit in these categories (salty, sweet, sour, savory, bitter, bland; don't forget crunchy, mushy, tough, tender, hot and cold).

Also gather blankets, paper plates, hats and sun screen, etc. Meet on the lawn or at a park and enjoy.

Talent Show

Babies can have a chance to show off to the other parents.

Using finger play books or activity cards, have each parent and baby team be prepared to perform a finger play or rhyme for the class.

Give awards for as many creative reasons as you can. Think of the *funniest, cutest, shortest, longest, most original, fastest, quietest, loudest, etc.*

TOPICAL INDEX: PIPE Activity Cards - Playing Is Learning

NOTE: Not all topics have corresponding activity cards

*Denotes suggested activities for demonstration

UNIT: Playing Is Learning

TOPIC: Play Is Imitation and Reciprocal Turn-Taking

0 - 5 mos.	5 - 10 mos.	10 - 15 mos.
1. Cooing Game	10. Sounds Baby Knows	19. So Big!
* 2. Listening and Answering	11. Toy Toss	20. Open, Shut Them
3. See and Say	12. Baby Rocks	21. This Is the Way
4. Mirror Talking	13. Play Dough Poke	22. Block Towers
* 5. Questions	*14. Crumpled Paper	* 23. Cars & Ramps
6. Wiggle Finger	* 15. Telephone Play	* 24. What Toy Is This?
7. Silly Sounds	16. Roly Poly Book	25. Sponge Fun
8. Tongue Fun	17. Pease Porridge Hot	26. Standing on One Foot
9. Who's Peeking At You?	18. Do What I'm Doing	27. High Jumping

© **Partners In Parenting Education 1994**

UNIT: Playing Is Learning

TOPIC: Playing While Learning About Differences

0 - 5 mos.	5 - 10 mos.	10 - 15 mos.
1. Texture Sticks	* 10. Three Toys	19. Fill and Pour
* 2. Roly Poly	* 11. Half Hidden	* 20. Stacking
3. Sit Ups	* 12. Sticky Ball Tape	* 21. Muffin Tin
4. This Hand and That Hand	13. Nesting Cups	22. MacDonald's Farm
5. My Baby Goes ...	14. Beginning to Scribble	23. Sink or Float
6. Pop Goes the Weasel	15. Bang, Bang Your Blocks	24. Stringing Beads
7. Bouncing Bear	16. Pie Tin Play	25. Pat-A-Cake
* 8. Painting Baby	17. Bumble Bee in the Barn	26. Pull Apart Toys
9. Sweet Baby of Mine	18. Rolling Cars	27. Puzzle

© **Partners In Parenting Education 1994**

TOPICAL INDEX: PIPE Activity Cards - Playing Is Learning

NOTE: Not all topics have corresponding activity cards

*Denotes suggested activities for demonstration

UNIT: Playing Is Learning

TOPIC: Playing Is Communicating

0 - 5 mos.
1. I'll Love You Forever
2. Did You Ever See a Lassie?
3. Two Little Blackbirds
4. Up Goes the Baby
* 5. Spider
* 6. Clap Your Hands
7. Ten Little Fingers
8. Are You Sleeping?
9. Here Are Your Ears

5 - 10 mos.
10. This Old Man
11. Knees and Toes
12. I'm a Little Teapot
13. Hickory,Dickory,Dock
* 14. This Is How
15. Turtle, Tiny Tim
16. Five Little Monkeys
* 17. Whoops, Johnny!
18. Five Little Mice

10 - 15 mos.
19. Teddy Bear, Teddy Bear
20. The Wheels on the Bus
21. Bubbles
* 22. Thumbkins
23. Touch Game
* 24. Little Turtle
25. Five Little Ducks
26. Three Little Monkeys
27. Baby Mice

© Partners In Parenting Education 1994

UNIT: Playing Is Learning

TOPIC: Playing Is Stimulation of the Senses

0 - 5 mos.
* 1. Pen Lighting
2. Feather Duster Fun
3. Texture Glove
4. Noisy Boxes
5. Patchwork Quilt
6. Color Strips
* 7. Finding Sounds
8. Telling Secrets
9. Spicy Socks

5 - 10 mos.
10. Sound Bottles
11. Spicy Socks
12. Jack In the Box
13. Picture Books
* 14. Spoon Friends
15. Touch Books
16. Drumming Fun
* 17. Paint Rolling
18. Xylophone

10 - 15 mos.
19. Taping Voices
* 20. Poke Box
* 21. Jingle Bells
22. Scented Play Dough
23. Texture Coloring
24. Color Paddles
25. Flashlight Fun
26. Read to Me
27. Spicy Socks

© Partners In Parenting Education 1994

About the Authors

The PIPE curricula was written as a volunteer effort. The authors are all professionals who work directly with parents and parent education in some capacity. It is their strong belief in the power of positive emotional communication that has led them to give their free time and their creativity to writing these three units.

Perry Butterfield, M.A., has been involved in research on emotional development in children for the last 20 years. She was an investigator in one of the initial research studies of Lay Home Visitation (1978) and has since been associated with R.N. Emde and the Program for Early Developmental Studies at the University of Colorado School of Medicine. Perry has also worked with families who have preterm babies and with the parents of blind and hearing-impaired children. As a consultant to the Teen Renaissance parenting class, she wrote and directed the videos on which the PIPE curriculum is based. She then joined forces with the educators who piloted her tapes, and she wrote the concepts and information pages for the curriculum. Perry did her undergraduate work at Smith College and her M.A. in Psychology at the University of Colorado, Denver. She interned with T. Berry Brazelton and Boston Children's Hospital. Perry is the mother of four children and grandmother to four more.

Sue Dolezal, M.A., is the Director of Program Development and is the originating director of Partners in Parenting Education. She secured the initial grant and supervised the survey of parent education materials. Sue developed the interactive method within the school setting and supervised the piloting of the PIPE materials in the classroom. She has designed and written many of the teaching strategies, interactive sessions, topic enhancers and evaluations for the Curricula. She is also the principal trainer for PIPE. For 20 years, she served as the parent educator and director of a school-based teen parent program in Brighton, Colorado. She has been a member of the Board of Directors of the National Organization on Adolescent Pregnancy, Parenting and Prevention (NOAPPP). She received a B.S. from Colorado State University in Home Economics education and her M.A. from the University of Northern Colorado in Adult and Community Education with a focus on parenting program development.

Barbara Pagano, M.A., developed the Teens Loving Children (TLC) program for the Cherry Creek School district in Colorado. Barb is the director and parenting educator for the program. She is the principal author of the teaching strategies for the *Playing Is Learning* curriculum. Barb earned her B.A. in Consumer and Family Education at the University of Northern Colorado and her M.A. in Early Childhood Education from the University of Colorado at Denver. She is on the Boards of the Aurora Teen Pregnancy Prevention Initiative, the Colorado Organization of Pregnancy, Parenting, and Prevention (COAPP) and How to Read Your Baby. Barbara conducted one of the original pilot programs for PIPE and has been using PIPE in her classroom for the last six years.

Authors & Contributors

Pilar Baca, M.S., R.N., is a Senior Research Assistant at the University of Colorado Health Sciences Center, Prevention Research Center for Family and Child Health, where she is the clinical supervisor for an intensive nurse home visitation program for high risk, first time mothers in Denver, Colorado. She also coordinates trainings nationwide on the Center's Pregnancy and Early Childhood Nurse Home Visitation Model. She has a long career in community and mental health nursing where she has worked with high risk families in acute hospital settings, in Head Start, and in correctional settings. Pilar is, herself, the single parent of a now grown son.

JoAnn Robinson, Ph.D., received her Ph.D. in Human Development and Family Studies from Cornell University. She is currently an Assistant Professor in the Departments of Pediatrics and Psychiatry at the University of Colorado Health Sciences Center. She is also the Research Director at the Prevention Research Center for Family and Child Health. Her publications are in the areas of early emotional development and parent-child relationships. JoAnn has been steadfast and creative in getting PIPE implemented in the Home Visitation 2000 research program. She has crafted their protocol for using PIPE and has worked with the training of home visitors in the PIPE method and concepts, and with documenting the effects of the PIPE program in this context. JoAnn has two children.

Gabriel and Jacinto Hernandez are brothers who have been working as free-lance artists for over five years. Their published credits include: "The Balls," a cartoon strip published in the *Rocky Mountain Collegian* (1991); *Lords,* a comic book published by Legend Comics (1993); "Joe Comics," a cartoon satire that appeared in National Lampoon March/April issue (1994); artwork published by How to Read Your Baby for *Love Is Layers of Sharing* (1995), *Playing Is Learning* (1997) and *Listen, Listen, Listen* (1998); and a "Joe Comics" cartoon strip appearing in *New Comics* issue #3 published by New Comics Productions (1997).